THE NATURE
AND
STRUCTURE OF
THE ISLAMIC WORLD

RALPH BRAIBANTI

THE NATURE
AND
STRUCTURE OF
THE ISLAMIC WORLD

Ralph Braibanti

James B. Duke Professor of Political Science Emeritus
Duke University

AFTERWORD
Javeed Akhter, M.D.

POSITION PAPER ONE

International Strategy and Policy Institute
Chicago, Illinois

First published 1995

Library of Congress Cataloging-in-Publication Data

Braibanti, Ralph J.D.
    The nature and structure of the Islamic world / Ralph Braibanti.
        p.   cm. -- (ISPI position papers ; no. 1)
    Includes bibliographical references.

    1. Islam--20th century. 2. Islam--Relations--Christianity.
    3. Christianity and other relations--Islam. 4. Islamic countries--
    Relations.   I. Title.   II. Series.
    BP163.B585   1995
    297'.09'o4--dc20
    ISBN 0-9647204-0-X
                                                                    95-19136
                                                                        CIP

Printed in the United States of America

CONTENTS

Oh believers: . . .
and hold fast all together by the rope
which Allah stretches out for you and
be not divided among yourselves; . . .

Holy Qur'an, III, 102, 103

THE NATURE AND STRUCTURE OF THE ISLAMIC WORLD

Ralph Braibanti

I

PROSPECTUS

The waning of the twentieth century has been characterized by the irrepressible effervescence of Islam. The
end of empire released powerful forces partially suppressed by colonialism. The effect of this explosion has
been global and profound, benign and sinister. It has
produced reactions of fear bordering on panic and hope
for the recovery and radiation of values held dear by
all civilizations.

During the past decade two new idioms affecting
the perception of Islam in the West have commanded
attention. The first, caricaturing Islam as the "Green
Menace" replacing the Soviet "Red Menace," is signifi-

cantly negative. The second is a slowly emerging recognition in ecclesiastical, intellectual and political circles of the theological validity and demographic, hence political, weight of Islam. This latter idiom is somewhat more positive in its effect. These two themes co-exist in a dialectical relationship. The dominance of one over the other cannot be clearly foretold. If militant radical trends among a minority Muslim group increase and expand spatially, then the emerging global respectability of Islam will be in eclipse. If these radical militant actions subside, a new globally-triumphal recovery of Muslim identity linked with spiritual growth and political influence could very well be the result.

These themes can be better understood by analysis of their content and by a survey of the structure of the highly complex world of Islam. The religious paradigm of the Muslim belief system has been exhaustively examined for several centuries in an enormous corpus of literature in many languages, hence no replication, or even summary, of that monumental bibliographic accretion is attempted in this essay. We seek instead to classify and evaluate elements of the paranoia towards Islam and to balance it with countertrends suggestive of a tranquil, constructive meeting of cultures. There then follows a tentative taxonomy designed to suggest an order for a complex world of ethnic, geographic, political variations united in a central theme of transcendental importance: Islam.

II

CIRCLES OF ANTAGONISM: POPULAR CULTURE

Antipathy towards Islam in the West has been well established as a daily ingredient in the media culture and as a recurrent theme in more serious instruments shaping opinion. At both levels, negativity and fear are the regnant idioms. In the realm of popular culture, especially in the United States, mean-spirited, often vicious distortions of Islam and Arabs have appeared with alarming frequency, increasing since the Arab oil embargo of 1977. Much has been written about such influence in the media;[1] a few contemporary examples demonstrate that themes of vilification have not disappeared.

Leon Uris' provocative book *The Haj* had a dustcover which styled the *J* in *Haj* as a scimitar, thus correctly foretelling its substantive contents.[2] The movie *Aladdin*, an animated feature film produced by the Walt Disney Studio, was the most financially successful animated film ever made. Released in 1993 in both theater and home video format, it had lyrics which originally read:

> Oh I come from a land
> From a faraway place
> Where the camel caravans roam
> Where they cut off your ear
> If they don't like your face
> It's barbaric, but, hey, it's home.

After meetings with the American-Arab Anti-Discrimination Committee, the fourth and fifth lines were changed to read:

Where it's flat and immense
And the heat is intense.

However, the word "barbaric" was not changed. Even the *New York Times* editorialized that the *Aladdin* lyrics were racist.[3]   Deploring "nasty generalizations about ethnic or religious groups," the *Times* editorial continued: "Thanks to current international politics, however, one form of ethnic bigotry retains an aura of respectability in the United States: prejudice against Arabs. Anyone who doubts this has only to listen to the lyrics in a song from the animated Disney extravaganza *'Aladdin'*."

One of the most bizarre characterizations of Arabs was the *New York Times* piece by Karl E. Meyer in 1992, which stated "The fanatic comes from the desert, the creator from the woods. That is the main difference between the East and the West."[4]

The documentary film *Jihad in America*, which was aired on the Public Broadcasting System in late 1994, characterized Muslims as bent on destroying American institutions. Muslim American leaders met representatives of all three major television networks at a press conference at the National Press Club in Washington, D. C. to denounce the "fiery rhetoric, unsupported allegations and spurious juxtapositions to build a case against Muslims in America."[5]

The 1994 movie *True Lies*, with Arnold Schwarzenegger in the lead role, is blatantly racist, anti-Muslim and anti-Arab. Movies slanted against Arabs or Islam are not a new phenomenon. *Time* magazine listed films starting with *The Sheikh* (1921), *Protocol* (1984) and *Jewel of the Nile* (1985)--all of which emphasized Arabs as exotic, sex-crazed lovers. *Lawrence of Arabia* (1962) depicts the Arab as "a political naif in need of tutelage from a wiser Westerner."

The Formula (1980), *Rollover* (1981) and *Power* (1981) emphasize the Arab as an unscrupulous, oil-wealthy plutocrat. *Black Sunday* (1977) and *Delta Force* (1986) portray the Arabs as terrorists.[6]

The most comprehensive and frightening treatment of Islam as a potential enemy of the United States is found in the work of Yossef Bodansky, former technical editor of *Israeli Air Force* magazine. Bodansky was staff director of the House Republican Task Force on Terrorism and Unconventional Warfare, chaired by Rep. Bill McCollum of Florida. The report of the task force viewed Islam as the successor to communism, aiming to "topple the Judaeo-Christian new world order." Bodansky, who, according to McCollum, was the author of this report, wrote a paperback book on the same subject after the World Trade Center bombing of February 1993.[7] The theme of the book is suggested in the author's preface: "Islamic terrorism has embarked on a Holy War, *Jihad*, against the West, especially the United States, which is being waged primarily through international terrorism."

Two subtle rhetorical aberrations further cloud our perception of Islam. The first is use of the term "fundamentalist" to describe those Muslims who engage in violence. This term is a transmutation from Christian thought where its meaning is well settled and precise. There it refers to those who believe in the literal, rather than the metaphorical, interpretation of the Bible, particularly the prophesies of the Old Testament. Most evangelical sects, the currently dominant portions of Southern Baptists (where there is a schism on this issue), followers of televangelists such as the Reverends Jerry Falwell, Jimmy Swaggart and Pat Robertson--all fit into this category. The criterion of belief in biblical inerrancy does not apply to a significant portion, probably a majority, of Christians. But in

Islam, all believers are fundamentalists. While there may be debate over some beliefs and practices, all Muslims believe in the sacred status of the Qur'an, i.e. that it was dictated by God through the Archangel Gabriel to the Prophet Muhammed and that the text has remained unchanged for some 1,400 years. To refer to those who commit acts of violence as fundamentalists is to insult the whole of the Muslim community. Further, it betrays either an abysmal ignorance of Islam or a deliberate effort to distort its image by linking violence to Muslims generally and to the quintessentials of their belief.

Closely related to this is the expansive use in Western media of the term "Muslim" to describe violent acts. Terrorism knows no religious or ethnic limitations. A few examples are illustrative of its universality and of the double standard used in the media for identifying its perpetrators. The Irish Republican Army, supported in part by contributions from Irish-Americans, has repeatedly bombed targets in London and elsewhere, fatally bombed Lord Mountbatten, and in 1992 alone killed or wounded 189 persons and permanently crippled 133 more by "kneecapping". Media accounts have not referred to these terrorists as Catholic. Terrorist acts against Muslims in India, especially in Kashmir, where tens of thousands have been tortured and killed, are not identified as acts by Hindus, nor are the killings of thousands of Muslims in Burma identified as Buddhist actions. The genocide, often by mutilation, rape and torture, of Bosnian Muslims (estimates are in the hundreds of thousands) does not label the perpetrators Orthodox Christians. The nerve gas attacks in the Tokyo subway in April 1995, allegedly committed by a group known as Aum Shinri Kyo has been referred to as a cult but not as a Buddhist cult. *The Wall Street Journal* of April 20,

1995, reporting on the bombing of the Federal Building in Oklahoma City, commented that there were two theories about who was responsible. The first suggested "Islamic extremists"; the second named "Branch Davidians". Since the first group was given a religious identity, the second should have been similarly labelled as "Christian". In all of these examples labels of nationality or of a non-religious group are used. Yet comparable acts by groups often not even declaring a Muslim identity are identified as Muslims. In recent years the terms "Islamist" and "Islamicist" have been used, presumably to distinguish varying degrees of militancy among Muslim groups. This adds to the confusion and perpetuates the problem of prejudicially applying a religious designation to abhorrent acts. The term "militant" is equally unsatisfactory when it is modified by "Muslim". The simple and correct solution would be to identify terrorists by nationality. Egyptian, Libyan, Iranian should be used in the same manner as Irish, Indian, Serb and Burmese. This would be a much more accurate designation since perpetrators of acts of violence, seldom practicing or pious Muslims, often use Islam as protective coloration. If such groups use the Muslim label in their name or announce their actions as a *jihad*, which is exclusively a Muslim term, then the media cannot be blamed for replicating this identification. When such a label is not used, it would be equitable to apply the same criterion as is used for non-Muslim violence, namely identification by country or by ethnicity.

Acts of violence against innocent victims are perpetrated throughout the world by a variety of groups. Those who commit these acts are a small minority of fanatical individuals whose acts are politically rather than religiously inspired. They are universally condemned by world and national authorities not least by responsible Muslim leadership. The alacrity with which public media jump to conclusions as to the source of violence is stunningly illustrated by the April 1995 bombing of the Federal Office Building in Oklahoma City. Government spokesmen warned against premature speculation about the identity of perpetrators. Despite this the immediate media reaction was to suspect Middle Eastern involvement. An American citizen of Jordanian ancestry travelling from Oklahoma City to the Middle East was apprehended in London and returned to the United States for questioning. He was released without prejudice though the only apologies came from television news broadcasters and talk show hosts. Within three days after the bombing an American citizen connected with a white supremacy movement was arrested and charged. This episode revealed not only the stereotyping of terrorism as Middle Eastern, but also exposed a whole range of sources of homegrown American terrorism.

The annual reports, *Patterns of Global Terrorism*, issued by the Office of the Coordinator for Counter-terrorism of the U.S. Department of State support this observation. In the reports for the five years from 1990 through 1994, 44 groups classified as terrorists are described. They include such entities as the National Liberation Army in Colombia, Sandero Luminoso of Peru, United Liberation Front of Assam, Chukaku Ha of Japan, New People's Army of the Philippines, Liberation Tamils of Sri Lanka, Red Army Faction of Germany, and Basque Fatherland and Liberty of Spain. Fourteen (31 percent) of these groups are said to have Middle Eastern connections. Three of these groups are avowedly Muslim; one, the Kurdish Peoples' Party (PKK), has no connection to Islam except that it is based in Turkey. The remainder are associated with

Palestinian liberation efforts. This list includes only groups engaged in international terrorism. If it included newly discovered domestic groups such as the Japanese Aum Shinri Kyo or American groups given notoriety by the Oklahoma City bombing, the percentage of Middle East-connected groups would be lower.

The reports for the 1990-1994 period show a total incidence of 2,096 acts of international terrorism. The greatest number, 695 (33 percent) were committed in Latin America. Except for one incident in Argentina in 1992 these were unrelated to any Middle Eastern or Islamic issue. Ranking next was western Europe with 648 (30 percent). There were 436 incidents (21 percent) in the Middle East. The remaining 16 percent of the incidents occurred in Asia (218), Africa (98), and North America (1). Some of the incidents in Asia and Europe had a Middle Eastern connection although the reports do not explicitly describe this. My own estimate would be that some 25 incidents in Europe and Asia had a Middle Eastern (perhaps Islamic) connection. This would only slightly increase to 21.1 percent the proportion of possibly Muslim-related incidents.

III

CIRCLES OF ANTAGONISM:
THE INTELLECTUAL IDIOM

The demonization of Islam is also a significant theme in more serious intellectual circles. Headlines of prestigious newspapers, magazine covers, the design of the book dustcovers as well as the substance of journal and news articles contributed to this distortion. A sample of such treatment is suggestive. As early as 1979

Peregrine Worsethorne wrote in the *Sunday Telegraph* of London:

Until this new threat from resurgent Islam is first understood in the context of the implacable motives behind it, which transcend reason and materialism and encompass religion, revenge and rage, can the proper and appropriate answers be found. Among those answers must be the possible use of armed force. For to encourage resurgent Islam to assume that it can get away with what amounts to a new style *jihad*, without its militancy being met by ours, this would condemn Christendom to an ignoble fate, as much invited as deserved. [*sic*][8]

In 1984, Amos Perlmutter who teaches at American University in Washington, D.C. and is editor of the *Journal of Strategic Studies* warned of "a general Islamic war waged against the West, Christianity, modern capitalism, Zionism and communism all at once. . . . [O]ur [the West's] war against Moslem populism is of the utmost priority, not the long term struggle against the Soviet Union."[9] Another influential analysis was the *Atlantic Monthly* article by the well-known historian of the Middle East, Bernard Lewis.[10] The word "rage" in the title of Lewis' article, "The Roots of Muslim Rage" had also been used earlier by the *Los Angeles Times* journalist, Robin Wright in her book, *Sacred Rage: The Wrath of Militant Islam*.[11] The evocative connotation of the term "rage" is self-evident. The eminent Russian novelist Aleksandr Solzhenitsyn similarly warned of the dangers to the West of a resurgent Islam.[12]

The covers of upscale periodicals have been another source of distortion. Two rather dramatic examples are illustrative. The November 19, 1990 issue of *The National Review* featured in bold half-inch headline type: "The Muslims Are Coming. The Muslims Are Coming." Thus there is evoked the slogan ingrained in American history and allegedly shouted by Paul Revere: "The British Are Coming." No less suggestive is the imagery of the popular movie "The Russians Are Coming." It cannot be lost on the reader that the British and the Russians were enemies of Americans and, by association, so must be the Muslims. Accompanying the headlines is a picture of an Arab camel race which can easily be construed as Arab warriors advancing in line of battle. Ironically, the article in the magazine, by Daniel Pipes, is moderate in tone and does not reflect the imagery of the cover. In a similar vein is the cover of the July 26, 1993 issue of *The New Yorker* which shows an Arab terrorist destroying a children's sand castle version of the World Trade Center in New York.

By far the most influential analysis of Islam as a probable enemy of the West is the seminal and provocative article, "The Clash of Civilizations?", which appeared in the Summer 1993 issue of *Foreign Affairs*.[13] The author, Samuel P. Huntington, is Eaton Professor of the Science of Government and Director of the John M. Olin Center for Strategic Studies at Harvard University. The significance of the article, sometimes compared to George F. Kennan's influential essay on containment of the Soviet Union, signed as "X" and published in a 1947 issue of *Foreign Affairs*,[14] was emphasized by an unusual publishing tactic. The September/October 1993 issue of *Foreign Affairs* included a 22-page   commentary on the essay by well-known analysts.[15] It was followed in the November/December 1993 issue with a response by Huntington.[16] This three-installment compilation continues to be available as a 57-page reprint. There are plans for publication of an expanded book version of this essay.

While the paradigm (a term not found in the original article but used in his subsequent response) constructed by Huntington embraced all civilizations, it emphasized Islam. Competition of political units in the world, Huntington said, will no longer be among nations, but between civilizations embracing groups of nations. These major civilizations include Western, Confucian, Japanese, Islamic, Hindu, Slavic-Orthodox, Latin American and "possibly" African civilization. The most provocative assertion is his characterization of the "Confucian-Islamic connection that has emerged to challenge Western interests, values and power." The danger of this nexus, he continues, is its reliance on nuclear, chemical and biological weapons, ballistic missiles and "other electronic capabilities" for delivering such systems. Specifically, he means North Korea and China (Confucian) and Pakistan, Iran, Iraq, Libya and Algeria. Although Huntington does not end his essay on an apocalyptic note, his policy suggestions clearly reveal a basic fear of the Confucian-Islamic nexus. He cautions that European, North American, Eastern European, Latin American and Russian civilizations must cooperate and must maintain military superiority. They must exploit differences and conflicts among Confucian and Islamic states and must limit the increase in their military strength. He moderates this Machiavellian stance by concluding that the West must understand the religious and philosophical underpinnings of these civilizations and must identify "elements of commonality" between them and the West.

The Huntington article was widely read, discussed and written about. The Muslim world was particularly upset by the assertion that the "Confucian-Islamic connection" poses serious security problems for the West.[17] The extent of its influence can be suggested by several Western references, some in accord and others in disagreement with the Huntington thesis.[18] Robert D. Kaplan, in his apocalyptic essay "The Coming Anarchy," modifying Huntington's analysis, reinforces the possibility of an Islamic clash with the West.[19] Kaplan admits that there are fissures within the Muslim world, particularly in the Fertile Crescent and the Caucasus. But environmental and demographic stress, added to Islamic militancy, cancels the effect of these fissures so that the Islamic threat to the West becomes more probable.

In the only footnote in his book, *Out of Control*, Zbigniew Brzezinski acknowledges reading the unpublished manuscript of Huntington's essay while his book was in press. He agrees with the fault lines and with the geographic element of the Huntington thesis in his own analysis of the "oblong of violence." He arrives at a much less pessimistic conclusion when he asserts that the "diversified Moslem world" is not ready to embark on war with the West and for America to act on that assumption would be "to run the risk of engaging in a self-fulfilling prophesy."[20] Former President Richard Nixon relates the Huntington thesis to current conflicts in Bosnia-Herzegovina and in Azerbaijan.[21] He warns against ignoring conflicts in which the Muslim world is victimized. In a sagacious comment he asserts that had Sarajevo been Christian or Jewish, the West "would have acted quickly and would have been right in doing so." Our failure to revoke the arms embargo against Bosnia "contributed to an image promoted by extreme Muslim fundamentalists that the West is callous to the fate of Muslim nations but protective of Jewish and Christian nations." While the Huntington prognosis may not be inevitable, Western (and especially American) policy may well result in a self-fulfilling prophesy.

One of the most carefully reasoned analyses of the alleged Muslim threat using Huntington as a point of departure is the feature article by Associate Editor Brian Beedham in *The Economist*. After criticizing Huntington's categories of civilization for being too rigid, Beedham denies the inevitability of a Muslim-West civilizational clash. The Muslim world can move confidently into the 21st century if it can solve three problems: coping with a modern economy, accepting the idea of sexual equality, and absorbing the principles of democracy. He makes a case for constructive mutual influence of Islam and the West. Using as a base those elements of commonality between the two cultures, Islam can influence the West to recover its belief in the "invisible life" and the West can help Islam to modernize. The two civilizations, he concludes, will not converge but they need "no longer regard each other as, respectively, amoral and fanatic."[22]

The commentary on Huntington's essay appearing in the *Foreign Affairs* issue following that of the original piece was uniformly a dissent. Civilizations are not watertight, states are more powerful than civilizations and indeed control civilizations, tradition weakens in the face of modernity. Other themes questioned Huntington's classification of civilizations, characterized Islamic "hegemony" as a myth, marked the powerful global force of democracy and the inevitability of the mixing and melding rather than the separation of civilizations.

My own analysis is in general agreement with this commentary, but some of the themes warrant further explanation. The formidable task of classifying, tracking and forecasting the fate of civilizations has challenged scholars for centuries. In modern times the 995-page *magnum opus* of Oswald Spengler: *Decline of the West*, first published in German in 1918 and in English eight years later, is a defining intellectual event.[23] Though the two terms are now used interchangeably, Spengler distinguished between "culture" and "civilization." Culture is the soul and civilization the intellect. Civilization emerges from culture; it is the destiny and the structure of cultures. This point is essential in understanding the changing nature of civilizations, which is my main criticism of the Huntington thesis. Spengler's schema embraces seven cultures: Faustian, Egyptian, Indian, Chinese, Classical, Arabian and Mexican. Like other analysts of civilization who follow him, Spengler pays special attention, in three chapters totaling 138 pages, to Islamic culture. This culture is the most self-contained, the most clearly defined, in which the "soul" is coterminous with the intellect, sentiment with structure; hence culture with its structural outgrowth: civilization. Spengler is the most influential philosopher of civilizations who makes this important distinction. The stimulating Russian thinker, Nicolas Berdyaev, in the Epilogue to his book, *The Meaning of History*, asserts that "great Russian thinkers of the past had already drawn the distinction between culture and civilization" and makes a brilliant, clear exposition of this distinction.[24] Arnold J. Toynbee, who refers to Spengler briefly by criticizing his organismic analogy to culture, uses the term "society". F.S.C. Northrop, making no reference to either Spengler or Toynbee, uses the term "society" generously and exclusively.

Toynbee's monumental *A Study of History* divides the world into 23 societies only five of which he found to exist at the time of his writing: Western Christendom, Orthodox Christian, Islamic, Hindu and

Far Eastern.[25] The contribution which Toynbee makes
to the study of civilizations is to direct attention to the
kaleidoscopic quality of change stunningly demon-
strated by the reduction of 23 societies to five. The
transformation of civilization is further explained by
his complex matrix of "culture radiation and reception," which establishes the concept that change in civilization is not unidirectional but is reciprocal and circular.

The seminal studies of Northrop are unfortunately
much less widely known than those of Spengler and
Toynbee. Northrop's aim, especially in his *The
Meeting of East and West*, is somewhat less metaphysi-
cally obscure than that of either Spengler or Toynbee.[26]
He seeks to overcome ideological conflicts by tracing
global problems to their roots and resolving them "in
theory, within the calmness of the study." This is un-
derstandable when we consider that the book was published in 1946, at the end of World War II, and at the
beginning of the Cold War with its threat of nuclear
annihilation. Northrop's catalog of civilizations is
more precise and clearer than that of Spengler and
Toynbee. It is free of the Teutonic and mystical underpinnings of the former and the rich, deep historical
context of the latter. The Northrop analysis is profoundly grounded not only in philosophic understanding of other cultures, but on intuitive comprehension
of what he calls the all-embracing, aesthetic continuum. He divides the contemporary world into seven
cultures: Islamic, Hindu, Latin American, Anglo-
American, Mexican, Western and Eastern (Oriental).
Like Spengler and Toynbee before him, especially like
Spengler, Northrop emphasizes the intuitive, artistic
and religious components of culture. Northrop carries
the earlier concepts of Spengler and Toynbee to a new
threshold by emphasizing the mutability of cultures

and the intricacies of their interrelationships. Acknowledging this, he seeks to find the ideological bases for their compatibility. He groups the seven cultures into two categories: East and West (hence the title of his book) by identifying religious and aesthetic complementarities. "It should be eventually possible," he concludes, "to achieve a society for mankind generally in which the higher standard of living of the most scientifically advanced and theoretically guided Western nations is combined with the compassion, the universal sensitivity to the beautiful, and the abiding equanimity and calm joy of the spirit which characterizes the sages and many of the humblest people of the Orient." This may appear to be an excessively optimistic view of civilizational change. Since it was written, there is evidence of both its validity and its weakness. The critical factor relating to the Huntington thesis is the inevitability of civilizational change so dramatic as to raise the possibility not of the clash but rather the accommodation.

Pitirim A. Sorokin, in his comparative analysis of the work of Spengler, Toynbee, Berdyaev, Northrop and others, finds concordance in their rejection of the linear concept of civilizational change.[27] In the evolution of civilizations there are oscillating variations, spiralling and branching development. This is further substantiation of the permeability of civilizational boundaries, a permeability which has phenomenally increased in the nearly half century since these works were written. Sorokin also distinguishes between culture and civilization: "civilizations...have shown a succession of cultural systems which cannot be described by the same label throughout their history as 'Greek civilization' or 'Western European civilization' without grave risk of misunderstanding and error."[28]

Other analysts confirm the difficulties in classifying civilizations and tracking their mutations. Studying West African societies as an anthropologist, Bronislaw Malinowski notes the circular change in cultures.[29] Norman Daniel, an historian using Islam as a case, distinguishes between culture and civilization. The latter he describes as the "achievement of civic skills."[30] Daniel refuses to attempt a taxonomy of cultures, maintaining that there are too many interconnections and that different generations are different cultures.

In sum, change is directed by the diffusion of norms and institutions and by conditions of receptivity in the receiving culture. When diffusion is reinforced by colonial rule and receptivity is enhanced by fragmentation and bewilderment of the receiving culture, the pace and depth of change are accelerated This analysis can be applied to the contemporary civilizations which Huntington describes. The diffusion of colonialism has been replaced by the dynamic of the technetronic and now cybertronic prowess of radiating societies. Recipient cultures have been bewildered by this unprecedented impact. Some, certainly Islamic cultures, try valiantly to resist such cultural intrusion, by re-asserting religious roots of the pre-technetronic age. Extremist minority groups sometimes resort to violence in a desperate attempt to stay the infiltration of norms deemed abhorrent.

Civilizational change cannot aptly be described by the geological metaphors of fault lines or plate techtonics. Civilizations are delineated by highly permeable membranes which filter norms and institutions circularly. The quality and rate of filtration depend on the viscosity of the substance being filtered, the force of radiation and the absorptive quality of receptivity. I have analyzed this process in some detail elsewhere and have illustrated it with a schematic diagram.[31] The distinction made by Spengler and others between culture and civilization is critical in understanding this process. Civilization--structures, artifacts, institutions, technologies--are filtered at one rate of speed. The almost immediate diffusion of television, nuclear power and other technologies are examples of this. But culture--the soul, the inward-dwelling, aesthetic quality of a people--may lag behind this diffusion. It penetrates the delineating membrane at a different rate of speed and may encounter different qualities of impedance. This is the theoretical explanation of the very real problem faced by Muslim societies. Eager to accept technological innovation, they facilitate its flow through the delineating membrane. But the culture of a radiating society meets resistance. Often the attempts to impede diffusion of culture while facilitating technological diffusion are frantic, even comic. Thus French efforts to keep its language pristine by demonizing "Franglais" and other efforts to control dress, tonsorial style and other "Western behavior," are impedances to contaminating influences. Unfortunately, these values (soul, culture) cannot be completely separated from technology (artifacts, civilization). They may flow through the membrane at different rates or may flow together in mixtures indiscernible to the recipient civilization. Every institutional and technological item, indeed every behavioral and attitudinal posture, is encased in a penumbra of epistemological premises from which it cannot be detached.

There is universal agreement among theorists of civilization that there is no static civilization. The immutable law of change applies to societies as well as to all units of existence. In our own time such change is especially rapid and dramatic. The civilization of

India is no longer dominated by the Gandhian ethic of *ahimsa, satyagraha* and *brahmacharya* which gave philosophical underpinning to the Indian independence movement. Within two generations India moved from Gandhian non-violence to the absorption of Kashmir and Sikkim, wars with Pakistan, a war with China, the acquisition of nuclear weapons and refusal to sign the nuclear non-proliferation treaty. Similarly Turkey in two generations changed from the Ottoman nominal leadership of the Muslim world to a secular state under a woman prime minister with an American Ph.D. It would be difficult to find more spectacular examples of rapid civilizational change.

Nor is the civilization of the United States the same as it was a half century ago. Gone is the ethic of Puritanism, religious and family values of a generation ago. The debate which dominates much of American, and to a lesser extent European, discourse centers on rapid change (some would say deterioration) of values which bond a society together. Muslim societies are horrified by the spectacle of the new Leviathan of culture, telecommunications, and technetronic imperialism which seems triumphant. Both of these anxieties are compelling proof of the circularity of civilizational change and the permeability of cultural boundaries.

IV

CAUSES OF ANTAGONISM

1. Contemporary Factors

The reasons for the West's unsympathetic reception of Islam are several. The most immediate cause can be found in the fear of rising Muslim violence spawned in the context of frustration over the plight of the Palestinians. This rationale has now been almost entirely displaced in Egypt, Algeria, Libya, Iran and Iraq by political discontent in contexts unique to each country. In the United States this image of Islam is reinforced by official policy towards Israel and the concomitant result that enemies of Israel must be regarded with suspicion. In Europe the roots of antagonism are essentially demographic. Germany, France, Austria and the United Kingdom are troubled by a massive increase of Muslims, first by immigration and now by the birth rate of domiciled immigrants.

The problem in France is more acute than in other countries because of former French colonial rule of Morocco and Algeria and the geographic proximity of these countries to France. The French see Islam as a threat to their culture. "We don't want France to become an Islamic republic," says Philippe de Villers, a member of the National Assembly. Charles Pasqua, Minister of Interior, has begun large scale deportation of illegal immigrants,[32] and pledges to close French frontiers and to reduce immigration to zero by the year 2000. France is concerned that the increase in population in Tunisia, Morocco and Algeria will produce a massive invasion. This is not to suggest that Pasqua is anti-Islamic, for he has also taken actions, mentioned later in this essay, which indicate an understanding and sympathy for Islam. His concern is the likelihood of France being overwhelmed by immigration, especially from North Africa. The fact that such immigration is Muslim is secondary to the issue of the magnitude of an impact too great for the nation to absorb. The novel *The Camp of the Saints*, first published in France in 1973, forecasts a cataclysmic invasion.[33] This novel by Jean Raspail was popularized in the United States by Matthew Connelly and Paul Kennedy in a bleak analysis of the global immigration problem appearing in *The Atlantic Monthly* in December 1994.[34]

The wearing of the *hijab* (head scarf) by girl students in French schools has been the precipitating event in antagonism towards Islam. The Ministry of Education banned the wearing of "all ostentational religious symbols in public schools." *The Conseil d'Etat* had ruled against the ban but in 1992 the Constitutional Council overturned the decision with an ambivalent verdict declaring the *hijab* compatible with the French ideal of secularism but banned any religious sign if the manner of wearing it was provocative. The Minister of Education determined that it was provocative; hence the ban. This decision has been attributed to a "wind of 'Islamaphobia' which is more serious in France than elsewhere in Europe."[35]

The Muslims in France number 4 million (1.2 million of whom are from Algeria) or 1/16 of the total population; the ratio in other European countries is much lower. The violence in Algeria generated by the frustration of Muslim groups deprived of their legitimately elected government and by the military coup which usurped power by nullifying that election was frightening to the French. That violence is associated with Islam generally. The problem is acerbated by the inability of the government to deal with some 600 Muslim organizations and with a Muslim population which, while predominantly Algerian, includes Muslims from some sixty countries. The current conflict is a legal problem of the relationship of the *Conseil d'Etat* to the Constitutional Council which can be resolved only by action of the National Assembly.[36]

The close geographical and cultural ties with Algeria have acerbated relations and there is suspicion that the agitation in France is supported if not caused by the Algerian National Salvation Front. The children of immigrants, now French citizens by birth, are demanding political rights. Organized into groups such as Young Citizens of France, they have turned to Islam as a political protest. The expulsion of some 88 girls from school for wearing headscarfs is especially troubling since Sikhs are allowed to wear turbans and Jews may wear skull caps (*yarmulke*). In December 1994 hijackers commandeered an Air France Airbus 300 in Algiers. En route to Paris the plane stopped to refuel in Marseilles where the hijackers killed three passengers and released others. French commandos stormed the plane, killed the four hijackers, released all the passengers and found about twenty sticks of dynamite beneath the plane's seats. It was thought the plane was on a suicide mission to explode in or over Paris. The next day, four Catholic priests, one of them Belgian, three French, were murdered in northern Algeria.

In Germany the focus is on unemployment, especially since unification. In Austria the attitude towards Muslims is merged into the larger problem of immigration, most of which is non-Muslim. Located on the frontier of Europe's immigration phenomenon, Austria has received and processed the bulk of refugees from the former Soviet Union and eastern Europe:

some 42,000 from Yugoslavia alone. Nearly half a million foreigners live in Austria whose population is 7.5 million. New immigration laws passed in 1993 make it difficult for immigrants to live and work in Austria. The backlog of applications for residence permits is some 60,000 and the long delay means that the applicants lose jobs, places to live and are forced to return to their places of origin. As in other European countries, the strict immigration policy enhances the standing of some politicians who advocate an end to all immigration.[37]

In Britain anti-Muslim sentiment arises from fear of British culture and institutions being overwhelmed by foreign immigrants (Indian, Pakistani, Bangladeshi, West African, West Indian) whose cultures are markedly different from that of Europeans. The Islamic dimension of this fear is subordinate to the issue of the magnitude and incompatibility of the new migration. To a lesser extent than in the United States, this sentiment gains some strength from the Zionist-Arab politics of the Palestine issue in which British policy played the determining role in 1948. The galvanizing event (analogous to the wearing of head scarfs in France) has been the matter of government support for Islamic schools. There is some feeling that this policy started with Sir Keith Joseph, a Zionist, who as Minister of Education maintained that Islamic education would contaminate the cultural purity of British education. This view has continued for there is no objection to support of Jewish, Catholic or Protestant schools. The British National Party's success in getting its candidate elected to the Borough Council of Tower Hamlets in London's East End was disturbing since the National Party Platform advocated forced deportation of all blacks and Asians. This election of September 1993 followed the beating into a coma of a 17-year old

Bangladeshi by a group of whites. In the context of 7,993 racial attacks reported for 1993--almost double the number for 1992--this election was viewed with alarm by Muslims.

2. Bedrock of Antipathy

Beyond these contemporary sources of antagonism lie deeply-rooted circumstances. It can justifiably be said that these 20th century feelings can be traced to the Crusades which generated a repugnance towards Islam in the 12th and 13th centuries. Dante's *Inferno* sentenced Mohammed and Ali to the ninth *bolgia* as dangerous sowers of discord and disunity (*seminator di scandalo e di scisma*). Mohammed was regarded as the figure who broke the hold of Christianity, hence was sentenced to the cruelest punishment described in the *Inferno*: being cleft from head to crotch. Allegorical though it was, the *Inferno* was undoubtedly a reflection of mediaeval thought.

Only six centuries after the rise of Christianity, Islam emerged incorporating some of the doctrine of its two Abrahamic predecessors, Judaism and Christianity, and claiming to be the ultimate divine revelation. Islam was, and continues to be activated, by a dynamic zeal for global propagation which directly confronted the same Christian impulse. The universality of Islam was threatened by this dynamism as Islam spread in Asia and Africa and to the very gates of Vienna, destroying the possibility of converting the whole world to Christianity.

The second factor, peculiar to American culture, is the phenomenal rise in the United States in visibility and authority of evangelical Protestant fundamentalist Christianity with its emphasis on the Old Testament and on "biblical inerrancy," i.e. the literal interpretation of Scripture as the infallible word of God. An important part of this view is the literal belief in biblical prophesy.[38] These views, persuasively propagated by televangelists, emphasize the special status of Israelites and Zion and warn that divine retribution will be meted out to whomever disagrees. The contemporary Israelis are equated with biblical Israelites, and their possession of Palestine is proof, according to this view, that a biblical prophesy has been fulfilled. These notions are coupled with what might be called the Judaization of Christianity, in which the Judaic antecedents of Christian doctrine and the Jewish genealogy of Christ and the Holy Family are given so much emphasis that the distinctions between the two religions are blurred. The theological and historical relationship between these two religions cannot be denied and should be explained and taught. But this view ignores the third Abrahamic religion, Islam, which has both Jewish and Christian roots. Thus Islam, marginalized, is seen as the enemy of both. Since these ideas touch the very essence of the Arab-Israeli problem, namely the status of Israel and Palestine, they are hardly conducive to increasing an empathy for Islam. The recent work of Fuad Sha'ban shows the depth of these beliefs and reveals a dimension which has been eclipsed or isolated from the political context in which Islam is immersed.[39] He shows that fundamentalist views of Zion are not new but are deeply embedded in American 19th century literary and religious sources. It is the millenarian attitude, enmeshed in Old Testament prophesy, which generated much of the pilgrims' euphoria inspiring the settlement of the United States. America became the Zion, the paradise, for the early settlers, later including the Mormons. This is reflected in the names given to thousands of towns throughout the United States: Salem, Sinai, Nazareth, Providence, New Jerusalem, Bethel, Mt. Olive, New Bethlehem, Zion, Hebron, Mt. Carmel, Mt. Hermon, Canaan, Mt. Pisgah, Nebo, Lebanon, Palestine, to name but a few.[40] Some of these names were given by settlers from Syria/Lebanon but most were bestowed by European settlers inspired by biblical references. The New Jerusalem of the early settlers' fantasy is materialized in the recreation of the Jerusalem of modern Israel. The relationship between this view of Israel and the consequent isolation of Islam is subliminal but remarkably influential in molding American views of Islam. These modified perceptions are strengthened by antecedent imagery of the Crusades against the infidel allegorized in the *Inferno* and are given new and stronger meaning by contemporary events which plunge them into the maelstrom of global politics. The consequence is that the emotional circumstances sustaining a western alienation with Islam are given new meaning and depth. American attitudes towards Islam and Arabs are not exclusively the consequence of the 1948 establishment of Israel, the Arab oil embargo, the Iranian hostage-taking or other violent events attributed to Islamic inspiration. They have much deeper roots.

V

CONSTRUCTIVE ATTITUDINAL CHANGE

Despite the negative influences consequent to the factors analyzed above, there have been several developments, especially during the last decade, which have improved the image of Islam. These changes have not yet overtaken the negative influences. That transformation depends to a great extent on the incidence of violent acts which, rightly or wrongly, are ascribed to Islamic sources.

The first change lies in the religious realm. Mainline Protestantism, Catholicism and Orthodoxy have abandoned earlier exclusionary views of other religions. The words "heathen" and "pagan" have disappeared both in hymns and official statements. Courses on Islam and other religions are now taught in major theological schools and significant ecumenical dialogue has occurred. The Old Testament literalism characterizing American Protestant evangelicals is not found in Europe or in mainline American churches. The statement of policy adopted unanimously by the National Council of Churches in 1980 is quite different from the fundamentalist's views and is similar to the carefully crafted positions espoused by Roman Catholicism since 1964.

Both the Roman Catholic and the Orthodox churches show a greater appreciation of Islam and an affinity with Arab culture. The existence of the Pontifical Institute of Arabic Studies and the policies enunciated by the Second Vatican Council, as well as the Twenty-Four Declarations issued by the Vatican-Muslim Conference in Libya in 1976, make this clear. The Roman Church embraces within its fold a variety of Eastern rites in some of which Arabic is the liturgical language. It is significant that the liturgies at the elevation of a new pope, the Pontifical Christmas Mass and the annual Pontifical Christmas message and blessing include some liturgical reading or message in Arabic. Ironically, the crusader legacy and the conquest of Spain, both occurring in the context of an undivided Christendom, have not resulted in a theological or institutional antagonism towards Islam in the Catholic

Church. The Vatican position, shared in large measure by Orthodoxy and by the Episcopal, Lutheran, Presbyterian and Methodist churches, is in stark contrast with the fundamentalist millenarian views discussed earlier.

There are several governing documents elucidating the Catholic change of perspective towards Islam. This change is linked to a somewhat different interpretation of the role of the missionary in non-Christian societies. Father Georges C. Anawati attributes much of the new perception of Islam to the influence of the distinguished French scholar of Islam, Louis Massignon, who had a long-standing friendship with Pope John Paul VI.[41] The Vatican's re-evaluation of Islam is of enormous significance in the evolution of Christian-Muslim relations. It reversed an attitude of antagonism which had existed since the Crusades of the eleventh and twelfth centuries. The documents parallel a similar point of view enunciated by mainline Protestant churches through the National Council of Churches. These views, both Catholic and Protestant, are bolstered by sympathy for the Palestinian cause, expressed in a variety of other statements. The papal documents referred to here, however, deal exclusively with Islam as a religion not to the political problem of Israeli-Palestinian relations. It should also be pointed out that the new attitude towards non-Christian religions includes Judaism, whose special historical and theological relationship to Christianity is acknowledged and admired. These new attitudes are deftly, brilliantly and almost poetically summarized in a series of brief essays by Pope John Paul II in his new book, *Crossing the Threshold of Hope*.[42] As early as 1964, following Vatican Council II, Pope Paul VI declared in *Ecclesiam Suam*, "We do well to admire these people [of the Moslem religion] for all that is good and true in their worship of God."[43] This was confirmed in his encyclical letter *Lumen Gentium*, "But the plan of salvation also includes those who acknowledge the Creator, in the first place among whom are the Moslems..."[44] It was Paul VI's encyclical declaration, *Nostra Aetate* which set forth this new relationship most clearly and fully:

The Church has also a high regard for the Muslims. They worship God, who is one, living and subsistent, merciful and almighty, the Creator of heaven and earth who also has spoken to men. They strive to submit themselves without reserve to the hidden decrees of God, just as Abraham submitted himself to God's plan, to whose faith Muslims eagerly link their own. Although not acknowledging him as God, they worship Jesus as a prophet, his Virgin Mother they also honor, and even at times devoutly invoke. Further they await the day of judgement and the reward of God following the resurrection of the dead. For this reason they highly esteem an upright life and worship God especially by way of prayer, alms-deeds and fasting. Over the centuries many quarrels and dissensions have arisen between Christians and Muslims. The Sacred Council now pleads with all to forget the past...[45]

Respect for Islam does not mean that the Catholic church has abandoned its missionary efforts. In *Evangelii Nuntiandi*, Paul VI reaffirmed keeping alive the missionary spirit which "never ceases" and that respect and esteem for such religions as Islam should not be interpreted as "an invitation...to withhold from these non-Christians the proclamation of Jesus."[46] A somewhat different attitude towards missionary activity, "a new evangelization" was first expressed in the encyclical *Ad Gentes* in 1965, amplified and confirmed by John Paul II in *Redemptoris Missio* in

1990.[47] This landmark document calls for inter-religious dialogue, profound understanding of the indigenous recipient culture ("inculturation"), and activity in social institutions such as schools, community projects and hospitals. Pope John Paul II has written in *Crossing the Threshold of Hope* that by the year 2000 Muslims will outnumber Catholics who then become the new minority. This statistic alone must not deter evangelization; rather, he continues, it can only engender greater determination to overcome obstacles.

In 1974 Paul VI established the Secretariat for non-Christians, with a special section to study Islam. Since that time meetings have been frequent. Is it possible that if Dante Alighieri were writing today we would find Muhammed in *Paradisio* rather than *Inferno*? There is also emerging a pattern of Catholic-Muslim cooperation in politics and diplomacy. Recent joint efforts in New York on blocking sex education measures in schools and defeating birth control provisions at the United Nations Conference on Population in Cairo are stunning examples. Muslims find themselves in agreement (except for the strictures against capital punishment) with the message in the encyclical of John Paul II, *Evangelium Vitae* of 1995.[48] This new understanding of Islam by Catholicism, resonant in mainline Christianity, and the compatibility of views on many social issues, portends a new harmony between these two religions.

In the political arena several changes favorable to a better perception of Islam can be noted. The increasingly sophisticated strategy of Muslim and Arab groups in the United States has been effective in countering much of the distortion. Among organizations now learning to use the strategies of other, particularly Jewish, groups are the Islamic Shura Council of North America, the Islamic Society of North America, the

American Muslim Council, the American-Arab Anti-Discrimination Committee, the North American Council for Muslim Women, the Council on American-Islamic Relations, and the Arab-American Institute. The latter has been especially effective in national politics and was able to get platform discussion of the Palestinian issue at the Democratic National Convention in 1992, the first time this has occurred.

The Middle East Policy Council, (founded originally as the American-Arab Affairs Council) publishes the highly respected journal *Middle East Policy* (formerly *American-Arab Affairs*), now in its thirteenth year of publication. The Council also conducts workshops on Islam and Arab Affairs for high school teachers throughout the country and holds seminars for members of Congress and their staffs. The National Council on U.S.-Arab Relations, is a flourishing organization with activities on several fronts. It has sent hundreds of high school seniors to the Middle East as Kerr Scholars. Under the Malone Fellowship Program, it has sponsored nearly four hundred college professors in the Middle East for short terms of study. Hundreds of college students have participated in model assemblies of the League of Arab States held in all parts of the country. Study trips to the Middle East have been arranged for college presidents, cadets in military academies, members of Congress and their staffs, journalists and public school administrators. There are also several successful Muslim organizations with intellectual objectives. The largest of these is the Islamic Society of North America with headquarters in Plainfield, Indiana. It serves as an umbrella organization for 521 Muslim professional and other societies and holds annual conventions attracting thousands of Muslims. The International Institute of Islamic Thought in Herndon, Virginia, has since 1983 published the influential scholarly journal, *The American Journal of Islamic Social Sciences.* The impact of these activities, both political and intellectual, is being felt in the United States.

The media have not been entirely negative in their appraisal of Islam. An editorial by Richard Cohen in the *Washington Post* of July 27, 1993 typifies a more reasoned attitude: "A fear of Islam is deeply embedded in Western culture. [We must] stop affixing labels to a vast religion (Islam) or a whole people (Arabs) whose diversity is stunning. They have their fanatics, of course, but before we throw stones of gross generalizations, we ought to check our own glass house." *The New York Times,* which took a similar position in an editorial referred to earlier,[49] later published several articles in serial form on "Islam in America" in May 2-7, 1993 issues. They were dispassionate in tone; indeed the analysis was somewhat like that of the issue of *The Economist* referred to earlier.[50] Secretary of State Warren Christopher, former Governor Mario Cuomo of New York and former Mayor David Dinkins of New York City have publicly denounced defamation of Muslims.[51] Robert H. Pelletreau, Jr., Assistant Secretary of State for the Middle East, has similarly cautioned against viewing Islam as a menace replacing the Soviet Union.[52] Richard Armitage, former Assistant Secretary of Defense and National Security Advisor Anthony Lake have taken strong positions against Huntington's thesis of the dangers of an Islamic threat.

Three of the most perceptive, most carefully balanced analyses are books by William Pfaff and John Esposito and the special issue of *The Economist* by Brian Beedham.[53] Pfaff regards the fundamentalist movement as essentially defensive and isolationist rather than expansionist. Since these Muslims are in flight from the West "[why] would they want to incorporate still more of the West and its civilization within their own religious frontiers?... They would not dream of attempting to overrun western societies even if that were possible." Esposito's analysis is somewhat different, but he also concludes that the perceived Muslim threat to the West is without foundation. Beedham's analysis was summarized earlier in this essay.

Other developments, largely ignored by the media, suggest a slowly changing attitude in the United States. The United States now has some 600 mosques serving 6 million Muslims. The American Islamic College was established in Chicago in 1981 with financing from the Organization of the Islamic Conference. In both the House of Representatives in 1991 and the Senate in 1992 a Muslim cleric gave the opening invocation. These were the first such events in the history of the Congress. In 1993 the first *imam* was commissioned a captain in the U.S. Army. The US. Navy plans to commission Legalman First Class Malik Noel as an imam-chaplain. The American Muslim Council, based in Washington, D.C., has become increasingly active in monitoring what it regards as anti-Islamic actions. It recently announced plans to register one million Muslims to vote in the 1996 elections. Recently it protested to the United Nations the unbalanced composition of the tribunal to try war criminals in former Yugoslavia. Even though most of the victims were Muslim, no Muslim was included on the ll-member tribunal. From Malaysia, a Hindu was appointed; from Pakistan, a Parsi; and from Egypt, a Christian. Yet all three countries are overwhelmingly Muslim. This protest, although it may have been ineffective, is another indication of the slowly growing political awareness finding institutional expression among Muslims.

In western Europe where some 15 million Muslims live and in the Russian Federation and Georgia with some 21 million there is some evidence to suggest that progress towards greater empathy for Islam is being made. Much of this is due to organizational sophistication of the Muslim communities and an increased awareness by non-Muslims of the significance of the global Muslim resurgence. In September 1993 the World Islamic Council sponsored a three-day conference in London on Muslims in the West which was attended by Muslims throughout the world, including Australia, Japan and the United States. This was not the first instance of such international cooperation. Scores of international symposia have been held in many countries under the aegis of the Organization of the Islamic Conference, League of Arab States, Muslim World League and similar organizations. The 1993 London conference reflected the emerging integration of Europe and the common problems of Muslim minorities in that area. The London meeting issued a 23-point plan which included establishing a Council on Shar'ia to decide conflicts in interpreting Islamic law.

In England the most heartening development mitigating the increase in racial riots mentioned earlier was the televised address of the Prince of Wales on October 27, 1993. It was given originally in the Sheldonian Theatre of Oxford University at the opening session of the Oxford Centre for Islamic Studies. Widely reprinted in the Arab world it was the basis for a television film shown in Britain. It was also the inspiration for an international conference held at Ditchley Park and convened by the Oxford Centre in October 1994. With uncommon eloquence and empathy, Prince Charles traced the contributions of Islam to western civilization. The most appealing theme was his view of the contribution which Islam can make to contemporary life:

Islam can teach us today a way of understanding and living in the world which Christianity itself is poorer for having lost. At the heart of Islam is its preservation of an integral view of the universe. Islam refuses to separate man and nature, religion and science, mind and matter and has preserved a metaphysical and unified view of ourselves and the world around us. . . . The West gradually lost this integrated vision of the world with Copernicus and Descartes and the coming of the scientific revolution. A comprehensive philosophy of nature is no longer part of our everyday beliefs.

The Crown Prince reiterated this view in a conference "Britain and the World" convened by the Royal Institute of International Affairs in March 1995. Even more enthusiastically received by Muslims was Prince Charles' separately televised comment that he would prefer to have one of the Crown's titles changed to "Defender of Faith" from "Defender of *the* Faith". He referred specifically to Islam as one of the faiths in England.

Another welcome development in Britain was implementation in July 1994 of a new syllabus for state schools which makes the teaching of the principles of Islam, Christianity and Judaism mandatory for students in elementary and secondary schools.[54]

There are other indications of a changing image of Islam in Europe. The second largest mosque in France was dedicated in October 1994 in Lyon, serving 300 thousand Muslims in the Rhone-Alpes region. The mosque, along with several others in France, was financed by Saudi Arabia. The dedication address was given by Interior Minister Pasqua who on previous occasions had advocated a ban on all immigration. Pasqua affirmed the French government's support of Muslims: "Today Islam is a French reality because it is the religion of a big portion of Frenchmen. And it is not enough to have Islam in France; we must have an Islam of France."[55] In October 1993 the first Islamic University opened in Paris with an initial enrollment of 300 students. Half of the courses offered are religious and fifteen percent are in Arabic. The university seeks to develop knowledgeable, practicing Muslims who can also be good French citizens. At the governmental level an auspicious point of view was expressed by Philip Sagan, speaker of the National Assembly. After tracing the mutual influences between French and Islamic culture, he concluded that the two cultures are closer to each other than is commonly thought.

In other European countries there are hints of positive developments. Europe's largest Islamic cultural center has been built in Rome. Opening in 1995, it includes a mosque for 2 thousand worshippers, a library, museum and conference room. Saudi Arabia has contributed seventy percent of the cost; other Muslim countries contributed the rest. Under the ageis of King Faisal the decision to build the center was made in 1972; construction began in 1984 with the personal encouragement of the President of Italy. The cultural center symbolizes the amicable relationship which has emerged between the Vatican and Islam. In Germany the state of Nordrhein-Westfalen in 1995 mandated the study of Islam in its primary, intermediate and secondary schools.

VI

STRUCTURE OF THE ISLAMIC WORLD

What is this world of Islam which has commanded so much international attention during the last half century and which has been demonized especially in the last decade? Here it is contended that a systematically constructed taxonomy does not lend support to the thesis of Huntington and others that Islam is a life-threatening monolithic danger to the West. It may be that certain countries with a Muslim population and professing an Islamic impetus may constitute a threat of some description. This can be ascribed to the interests of particular nation-states rather than to a global or even regional Muslim conspiracy. China and North Korea pursue a foreign policy not because they are Confucian but because they must protect their national interest. Pakistan pursues its foreign policy because of a perceived threat from India not because it is Muslim.

While it is a risk to attempt to describe a phenomenon of the magnitude, diversity and complexity of the Muslim world, some typology, no matter how hypergeneral, is essential.

1. The Ummah - A Global Reach

With a population somewhat more than one billion or some 27 percent of the world's population, belief in Islam is spread in every conceivable geographical and political configuration--ranging from Morocco to the Sultanate of Brunei Darussalam (pop. 285,000). No other religion has quite so powerful an impetus for global expansion--neither Buddhism, Hinduism, Judaism nor Christianity. The concept of world-wide

Christian unity, once a powerful force, has been eroded by sectarianism, schism, nationalism, secularism and by a loss of confidence in what once was regarded as the true faith.[56] From a Muslim perspective, the ecumenical impulse which aims toward a recovery of Christian unity so trivializes and neutralizes the pristinity and clarity of doctrine that the Christian zeal for conversion disappears. Agitation in the Church of England in 1984 over the consecration as Bishop of Durham of Dr. David Jenkins, who expressed disbelief in the Virgin Birth, a central doctrine of Christianity, dramatizes the dilemma of non-Orthodox Christendom in preserving the pristinity of doctrine. In non-Catholic and Orthodox Christianity the doctrine of Biblical "inerrancy" continues to compete with widely spread notions which limit scriptural significance to non-literal or metaphorical interpretation.

The recovery of Islamic identity stimulated by decolonization following World War II and the oil wealth of the Gulf, particularly that of Saudi Arabia, is statistically and visually evident throughout the world. The building of thousands of mosques, establishment of major Islamic universities (such as at Islamabad and Kuala Lumpur), printing, translation (even into Zulu) and distribution of millions of copies of the Qur'an, the herculean enlargement of the mosques at Makkah and Medina including installation of the world's largest air conditioning system, are suggestive of this phenomenal growth. Much of this resurgence is due to the financial support of Saudi Arabia. The rate of conversion to Islam is ominous to many. When the encyclical *Redemptoris Missio* was issued in 1991, Vatican spokesmen said it "reflected fears that Catholicism was lagging behind Islam in expansion in Asia, Africa and the Middle East."[57]

2. Solidarity or Fragmentation

A strong sense of fraternal bonding of all Muslims has been both a fantasy and an ideal but seldom a reality in Muslim history following the Prophet's death in 633 A.D. This quest for community is expressed in the concept of *ummah* (community of believers) and continues to be given rhetorical expression in contemporary Muslim affairs. The fact that it is mentioned in the Qur'an several times gives it a sacred position. It is similar to the Roman concept of *civitas* especially in its emphasis on putting the community good above personal desire and in directing the community towards virtue and away from evil. *Ummah* is an architectonic idiom whose purpose ultimately is to embrace all mankind. It is the external structural manifestation of the soul of Islam. That soul resides in the Qur'an, the *sunnah* which is a group of *hadith* which are sayings and opinions of the Prophet. These, together with *qiyas*, opinions of learned Muslims, and *ijma*, consensus of Muslim scholars, constitute the core of belief which sustain the *ummah*.

Ideologically the Muslim world senses a profound communion which has not been suppressed in the Muslim psyche; it continues to exist as a powerful primordial sentiment. The great German historian Oswald Spengler, who understood the mystical, intuitive components of man's nature, reminds us that the "Islamic community...embraces the *whole* of the world-caverns, here and beyond, the orthodox and the good angels and spirits, and within the community, the State only formed *a smaller unit of the visible side,* a unit, therefore, of which the operations were governed by the greater whole."[58] This impulse toward Islamic unity is also nurtured by a vivid memory of Islamic imperial grandeur and by a vibrant, dynamic of missionary zeal. The force of *ummah* is the tacit dimension, the psychic indwelling nature of Islam. The separation of Muslims into distinct, often mutually antagonistic, nations is a reality which does not fit comfortably in fantasies of a Muslim perception of world order. Nevertheless, it is not likely that a unified superstructure of Muslim states will supersede sovereign nation states in the foreseeable future.

The abolition of the caliphate by Kemal Ataturk in Turkey in 1924 marked the formal end of what by then had become only an empty shell of global unity. Iran, Egypt, Morocco, and Turkey had existed for centuries as discrete, rich civilizations with relatively fixed boundaries. Saudi Arabia was not a unified political entity until 1932. Together with Syria and the rest of the Arabian peninsula it had cartographic recognition as early as 1471 AD as *Arabia Felix*, *Ayaman*, *Petrea* and *Arabia Deserta*. The huge Ottoman Empire was divided by the Allies in 1923 into colonies, spheres of influence, mandates or trucial states, all with boundaries based on colonial politics, sometimes whims. Thus the future Muslim nation-states of the Middle East were born and the concept of *Ummah* eroded. In Asia and Africa, imperial policies demarcated the boundaries of the colonies of Britain, France and the Netherlands even as recently as the 1947 partition of India. The arbitrariness of national boundaries with minimal, often no regard for ethno/linguistic or geographic considerations continues to plague Muslim states and is often the cause of conflict. The establishment of Israel in 1948 and the irredentism of the Israeli state is the most glaring instance of colonial injustice and arbitrariness. It has been the primary cause of Muslim unrest and conflict within the Muslim world and in international relations. Decolonization following World War II spawned such independent Muslim states as Indonesia, Pakistan, Malaysia, Morocco, Tunisia, Jordan, Libya, Iraq, Syria and the Gulf States. Subsequently others such as Bangladesh, Brunei, Bosnia and the six Central Asian republics became sovereign entities. By 1994 the number of Muslim states had reached 52. The concept of the nation-state thus further eclipsed the vestigial remnants of global Muslim unity.

A major division of the *ummah* is that of Arabs and non-Arabs. Arabs constitute only 20 percent of Muslims; the largest concentrations are in such non-Arab states as Indonesia, Pakistan, Bangladesh and the Muslim minority of India. The most populous Arab country, Egypt, with about 60 million, is dwarfed by Indonesia's population of 250 million and the populations of Bangladesh (176m) and Pakistan (128m).

A strong sense of Arab solidarity had been pushed forward by the Pan-Arab movement of Egypt's Gamal Abdul Nasser as early as 1955, provoked further by the Suez War of 1956. For a few years this was a re-markably popular cause although limited to the Arab states whose population was a minority in the Arab world. We can label this the *Ummah Arabiya* in con-trast with the all-embracing *Ummah Islamiya*. The Pan-Arab movement was directed primarily against Zionism, imperialism and feudalism. It took a step towards political unity by Egypt's forming with Syria the United Arab Republic (UAR) in 1958. A few months later Yemen joined the UAR in a federated ca-pacity labelled the United Arab States. A military coup in Syria in 1961 forced Syrian withdrawal and the UAR collapsed. In 1964 Iraq and Egypt issued a proclamation establishing an Arab Socialist Union. There were simi-lar Egyptian efforts to federate with Sudan, and, in 1973, with Libya. None of those Pan-Arab overtures materialized. Jordan attempted a federative relationship with Iraq in 1958, but this too ended with the Iraqi Revolution of July 14, 1958. The fragile nature of these shifting alliances is evident in the different configuration of the Gulf War of 1991: Egypt and Syria against Iraq; Yemen and Jordan against Egypt.

Beneath the shifting cleavages that emerge in the Islamic world, there has come into being a global structure of considerable sophistication. There is a reciprocal relationship between the structure which arises from sentiment, even fantasy, and the depth of sentiment given institutional support. This embryonic infrastructure supporting the *ummah* is perennially disrupted in part by its own intra-Islamic disputes (Yemen-Egypt; Iran-Iraq; Iraq-The Gulf, Jordan, P.L.O., Iraq, Yemen-The Gulf) but in part also by non-Islamic forces experienced in techniques derivative from a doctrine of *divide et impera* as well as from Byzantium and Machiavelli. The sense of Arab unity institutionally expressed by these unsuccessful structures and by ideological movements such as the Baath Socialist party finds contemporary institutional expression in the League of Arab States (LAS), established in 1945, which now has a membership of 22 Arab nations. There are many other pan-Arab entities, including the Arab Fund for Economic and Social Development, the Arab Investment Company, the Special Arab Fund for African Development, Kuwaiti Fund for Economic Development and the Abu Dhabi Fund for Arab Economic Development.[59]

The intra-Arab differences over the Gulf War have undoubtedly weakened what little effectiveness the League of Arab States has had in recent years. It has successfully mediated some disputes but its inability to act against Iraq for its invasion of a fellow member state, Kuwait, was a defining moment in loss of prestige. The invasion was a clear violation of Article 2 of the Joint Defense Treaty which was part of the League's charter. It specified that armed aggression against any member was an action against all members and was to be repelled by collective or individual state effort.

In December 1994 a three-nation Arab summit was held in Alexandria. Egypt, Syria and Saudi Arabia reaffirmed their support of Syria's position on peace talks with Israel. This statement followed Syria's complaint that such Gulf states as Oman and Qatar were making overtures towards peace with Israel. Thus the divisions of the Gulf War and the Arab-Israeli peace negotiations continue to plague Arab solidarity, to weaken Arab international entities and to encourage the formation of smaller groups of Arab states with common, although often transitory national interests.

The most effective regional Arab organization is the Gulf Cooperation Council (GCC), formed in 1981 by six nations of the Arabian peninsula: Bahrain, Kuwait, Oman, Qatar, Saudi Arabia and the United Arab Emirates. Its importance has increased as a consequence of the Gulf War. In addition to extensive patterns of trade relations, its mutual defense policies have drawn the Gulf states, already bonded by geography and a common culture, more closely together. The last GCC annual summit of heads of state held in Bahrain in December 1994 suggests some of the problems faced by the region. Its joint communique strongly condemned violence and extremism whatever the sources. The report of King Fahd of Saudi Arabia to the Council, as chairman of the previous (14th) term, spoke of new regional defense and economic groupings in the world. He urged stronger economic ties leading to a Gulf common market and increased cooperation in defense arrangements. Peter Mansfield's use of the expression *New Arabians* as a book title is fortuitous.[60] The commonalities of the

Gulf states, especially their contiguity and economic circumstances, set them apart from other Arabs; this title deftly catches that separateness. The rather dramatic success of the Gulf Cooperation Council is suggested by the extensive body of published research which has been done in the short span of its fourteen-year existence.[61]

Although there has been much rhetoric about Arabs solving Arab regional problems, none of these agencies has been capable of dealing with the Iran-Iraq War, the Gulf War or the Palestinian problem. An Arab infrastructure (*Ummah Arabiya*) thus exists but has not yet been able to compete successfully with the nation-state.

Beyond the circle of the *Ummah Arabiya* is the Organization of the Islamic Conference (OIC), established in 1969 under the aegis of King Faisal of Saudi Arabia. This was the triumphal culmination of Faisal's life-long efforts towards global Islamic solidarity.[62] The catalytic event was the burning of the *Al-Aqsa* mosque in Jerusalem which was then under Israeli control. The first summit meeting of heads of state was convened in Rabat in September 1969. Although boycotted by Syria and Iraq, 25 Muslim states were represented; Iraq and Syria joined soon after. The first summit was followed in 1970 by the first conference of Islamic foreign ministers in Jeddah.

Summit meetings of heads of state have been held in Rabat (1969), Lahore (1974), Makkah and Taif (1981), Casablanca (1984), Kuwait (1987), Dakar (1991) and Casablanca (1994). The current membership was recently increased to 52 after the admission of four Central Asian republics (Azerbaijan, Turkmenistan, Kyrgyzstan and Tajikistan) formerly part of the Soviet Union. Bosnia-Herzegovina was admitted to observer status at the 1994 Casablanca summit and other states have a applied for similar status. Heads of state meet at summits every three years and there are annual meetings of foreign ministers who set the agenda and elect the secretary-general. The secretariat in Jeddah has a staff of about 150 officials from all over the Muslim world. When affiliated organizations such as the Islamic Bank are included, the total staff approximates 1,500. Established with a primary objective of securing Arab control of Jerusalem, its diplomatic and other activities have broadened far beyond that. It has established four international Islamic universities in Malaysia, Bangladesh, Uganda and Niger. These, together with the International Islamic University in Pakistan, are the major Muslim universities which now total twelve scattered in various countries.

The OIC rotates appointment to the post of secretary-general among the regions of Asia, Africa, the Middle East and Europe. A propitious tradition of leadership was started with the appointment of Tunku Abdul Rahman, former prime minister of Malaysia. He was followed by Hassan Tohami of Egypt, Amadu Karim Gaye of Senegal, Habib Chatty of Tunisia, and Syed Sharifuddin Pirzada of Pakistan. The current secretary-general is Dr. Hamid al-Gabdi, former prime minister of Niger. All have served with uncommon distinction. The post of four assistant secretaries-general has similarly rotated among various Muslim states. The selection of these officers, and the choice of geographically dispersed sites for summit and foreign ministers' conferences, suggests the importance of non-Arab Muslim states from all the continents and the reinvigorated sense of identity of Asian, African and Middle Eastern Islam. The OIC has achieved several diplomatic successes within the ambit of Muslim brotherhood. At the Lahore summit of 1974 Pakistan and Bangladesh were reconciled after their bitter war of secession. The 1987 Kuwait summit defused (with the cooperation of the Gulf Cooperation Council) the coup in Sharjah. Strenuous efforts to mediate the Iran-Iraq War undoubtedly helped in its ultimate resolution. Equally vigorous diplomatic activity sought to resolve the Soviet-Afghan War and the Gulf War. The 1994 summit declaration, condemning terrorism in all its forms, reaffirmed that terrorism contravened the values and traditions of Islam. That summit, attended by President Alija Ali Izetbegovic of Bosnia, gave special attention to Bosnia but recommended bilateral action by Muslim countries rather than pan-Islamic intervention.

One of the most significant ideological consequences of the OIC was King Faisal's call for greater understanding between Christianity and Islam. Faisal's ambition to establish constructive relations with the Vatican[63] was pursued after his death. This attitude towards cooperation with Christianity evolved at almost the same time as the Vatican's empathetic recognition of Islam discussed earlier.

The *Ummah Islamiya* can be divided into distinctive regional entities with common economic problems and, in some cases, cultural affinity. Reference has earlier been made to the Gulf Cooperation Council, by far the most successful of these regional groups. The Maghreb Union, established in 1989, consists of Morocco, Algeria, Tunisia, Libya and Mauritania.[64] A different national configuration is the Arab Cooperation Council also established in 1989, consisting of Jordan, Iraq, Egypt and Yemen.[65] Conflicting alliances during the Gulf War and the civil war in Yemen virtually collapsed this organization. A regional entity of ten countries, established in 1993 as the Economic Cooperation Organization, is made up of Iran, Turkey, Pakistan, Afghanistan and the six Central

Asian states of Azerbaijan, Turkmenistan, Uzbekistan, Kyrgyzstan, Tajikistan, and Kazakhstan. The potential economic and political power of this group is great but its effectiveness is handicapped by the rivalry of Turkey, Iran and, although not a member, Saudi Arabia for influence in Central Asia. It's third annual summit was held in Islamabad in March, 1995.

The distinctive character of Islam in East and Southeast Asia is reflected in the formation in 1993 of the Asian Islamic Council based in Colombo, Sri Lanka. Organized with the help of Saudi Arabia, the Council has predominantly a religious and cultural emphasis and includes representatives of Muslim states such as Indonesia and Malaysia and of minorities in the Philippines, Korea, Japan and other Asian countries. Hence its composition is that of individuals rather than the governments of nation-states. In this respect, as well as in its religious and cultural objectives, it resembles the Muslim World League more than the other regional entities described above.

Complementing the vigorous political and diplomatic activities of the OIC is the Muslim World League (*Rabitat al-Alam al-Islami*) also established by King Faisal in 1952 based in Makkah. This is a quasi-official body designed to coordinate and stimulate religious, cultural, youth, welfare and public service organizations--both national and international--throughout the Muslim world. Its periodic world congresses are attended by representatives of some 300 Muslim organizations. For many years, its secretary general was Dr. Abdullah Omar Naseef, a former president of King Abdul Aziz University and currently Vice President of the Consultative Council (*Majlis Al-Shoura*) established in 1993 as the supreme legislative body of Saudi Arabia. Dr. Naseef was an uncommonly effective leader who travelled extensively in behalf of Muslim causes. It was he who took the unprecedented action of addressing the annual convention of the Southern Baptist Association thus furthering King Faisal's objective of strengthening relations between Christianity and Islam.

One of the most promising activities of the Muslim World League was the establishment in 1987 of the Islamic Fiqh Academy. This is an effort to announce rulings in Islamic law (*Shari'a*) in such matters as human reproduction and other ethical issues. Since there is no central global authority to reconcile doctrinal differences or to issue edicts (*fatwa*) which have pan-Islamic validity, the Fiqh Academy is regarded as a move in that direction. *Fatwa* are issued on various problems from time to time by Sheikh Abdul Aziz bin Baz, President of Scientific Research, Islamic Ruling, Call and Guidance, but they apply only to Saudi Arabia. Some rulings carry moral authority outside the Kingdom. For example, in 1989 Iran called on Muslims everywhere to execute Salman Rushdie, author of *The Satanic Verses*, regarded by all Muslims as blasphemous. But the Muslim League, through the Fiqh Academy, called this decree inconsistent with Islamic values. It advocated instead a trial for Rushdie and a chance for repentance if found guilty. While this in no way invalidated the Iranian position (according to Iran), it does suggest a beginning effort to make Islamic policy of global applicability.

The foregoing suggests that an elaborate network for an Islamic global political structure has slowly emerged during the last few decades, but that its organization is loose and without central authority. The principal impediments to the emergence of a more effective universal Islamic community are the conflicts within Islam, acerbated by the Gulf War and by the intervention of foreign powers who view the rise of an effective Muslim power block as inimicable to their interests.

3. Muslim Minorities (*Dar al-Harb*)

The traditional way of describing the structure of the Islamic world is by dividing it into *dar al-Islam* and *dar al-harb*. The former, usually translated as the domain or realm of Islam, referred to lands ruled by Muslims or in which Muslim institutions flourished. The latter term: lands, domain or realm of war, referred to countries with non-Muslim governments. The two terms have also been translated as "Realm of Belief" and "Realm of Disbelief". *Dar al-Islam* embraces those states which declare themselves constitutively to be Islamic (such as Pakistan and Saudi Arabia). It also includes those where a majority of the population is Muslim although no official declaration of Islamicity has been made (Indonesia). These regimes are easily identified; they are the 52 member states of the Organization of the Islamic Conference listed in the appendix at the end of this essay.

The second category, *dar al-harb*, can perhaps no longer be appropriately thought of as a political context of warfare. It is more accurate to refer to this group as Muslim minorities living in a relatively peaceful non-Muslim regime in which their Islamicity can be fully and freely expressed. No doubt Bosnians, Chechyns as well as some Muslims who, viewing certain restrictions on their behavior in France, England and certainly in the former Soviet Union, might consider the traditional translation more accurate.

It may be useful to suggest a third category of refugees or migrants who have fled an unfriendly regime (Afghanistan, Palestine, Bosnia) but who have not established a permanent or semi-permanent home in their new land. This includes those who are refugees remaining in their own country such as the million Azeris in Azerbaijan, Biharis in Bangladesh, Afghans in Afghanistan, Chechyns in Chechnya or Muslims in Bosnia. All such refugees, whether outside or within their homeland, can appropriately be called *dar al-muhajirin* (realm or domain of refugees). There would inevitably be some overlap between this category and minorities. The distinction would be either the fact of an established new abode or the intent to remain in it. This group is not represented in any formal organization such as the OIC or the League of Arab States.

Cutting across all three categories is the conventional distinction between Arabs and non-Arabs. Arabs constitute some 20 percent of the Muslim world. They live predominantly in the 22 nations which are members of the League of Arab States listed in the appendix to this essay.

Minorities living in *dar al-harb* make up about one third of the world's Muslim population. Although relevant data are conflicting and imprecise, some approximations may be ventured. The largest concentration of minorities are the 130 million Muslims in India, constituting about 12 percent of the total Indian population. Before the break up of the Soviet Union, some 15 percent of the population was Muslim. With the independence of the Central Asian Muslim republics the Muslim minority in Russia has been reduced to about 3 percent. China has a Muslim minority of 40 million or 4 percent of the population. In South Africa, Muslims constitute 3.5 percent of a total population of about 40 million. For the whole of Southern Africa, Muslims are 20 percent of the population.

The minorities in Europe have been discussed earlier in this essay in the context of anti-Muslim sentiment. The smallest Muslim minority is that of Japan where 0.9 percent of the population follows Islam. In many states Muslim minorities are geographically dispersed. In others, such as China, Kashmir and the Philippines they are concentrated in a defined area determined largely by historical forces. In such instances they may constitute a majority in that specified territory (state or province) even though they are a minority in the nation as a whole. Of all the Muslims living in *dar al-harb* only the Muslims of the southern Philippines, Kashmir, Cyprus, Bosnia and to a lesser degree Eritrea, have sustained consistent dissonance with the majority regime over a period of years. Only Eritrea (once a part of Ethiopia) has successfully gained independence. The Republic of Northern Cyprus has achieved *de facto* independence but its *de jure* status has been recognized only by its sponsor, Turkey. The grievances of Muslims elsewhere, particularly in Europe are increasing but there are no moves for separateness.

Only recently has much systematic attention been given to the roles of Muslim minorities.[66] The Institute of Muslim Minority Affairs was established in 1976 at King Abdul Aziz University in Jeddah. Its excellent journal continues to be published in London. International seminars on minorities have been held in London in 1978 in Sherbrooke, Canada in 1981 and in Perth, Australia in 1984. A growing body of literature is emerging and an international body of specialists in Muslim minority problems has emerged with communication links and publishing outlets. The World Islamic Council for Propagation and Relief convened a seminar in London in January 1995 on minority problems. These developments will strengthen Muslim identity within each minority and may ultimately affect the manner in which Muslims as minorities are treated in the non-Muslim states where they live. What is now needed is formal representation of minorities in such institutions as the Organization of the Islamic Conference. Whether or not new Muslim states will be created by secession or by boundary changes remains to be seen.

4. Refugees (*Dar al-Muhajirin*)

The problem of Muslim refugees which I have labelled *dar al-muhajirin* has received even less attention than minorities. Although the figures fluctuate rapidly, it is estimated that the number of refugees in 1994 approximates 23 million.[67] Although it is impossible to determine accurately, my estimate would be that approximately 80 percent or about 18 million, are Muslims. The volatility of this figure is suggested by the fact that in early 1995 it was increased by more than 300 thousand Muslim refugees who fled Grozny, Chechnya as a result of Russian military action there. The largest group of Muslim refugees were the Afghans (some 5.7 million) who fled their country for Pakistan, Iran, Iraq and elsewhere. The oldest and second largest group are the Palestinians numbering about 2 million, concentrated in Jordan, the West Bank and Gaza but scattered in a global diaspora. Bihari Muslims trapped in Bangladesh because they are Urdu-speaking citizens of Pakistan number about 200 thousand.

Refugees have a special status in Islam since the Prophet himself as a refugee fled from Makkah to Medina.[68] From that date, 622 A.D., the Muslim calendar begins. The living significance of this tradition is suggested by the comment of Brigadier Said Azhar who was Pakistan's Chief Commissioner for Refugees: "Pakistan's humanitarian gesture is influenced by various Qur'anic injunctions on the treatment of migrants who forsake their homes for the sake of Allah. It is against this background that the people of Pakistan have shared property and poverty in the noble spirit of the first migration (*hijra*) of Muslims from Makkah to Medina 14 centuries ago."[69]

5. Cultural Diversity Within A Universal Islam

The quintessentials of Islam command universal acceptance but the behavior and practices of Muslims living in distinctive political-cultural configurations differ. Certainly it can be said that all profess to believe in such canons as the absolute oneness of God (*Taw'hid*), the sacral status of the Holy Qur'an revealed by God through the Archangel Gabriel to the Prophet, the belief that there can be no prophet after Muhammad (Seal of the Prophet) and the Five Pillars of Faith: testimony of faith (*Shahadah*), prayer five times daily (*salah*), fasting during the month of *Ramadan* (*siyam*), tithing of income for charity (*zakah*) and pilgrimage to Makkah (*hajj*), . The universality of these beliefs cuts across sectarian lines such as Sunni and Shia and, (except for the Seal of the Prophet), are embraced even by such a sect as the Ahmadiyyas who are regarded by Pakistan, Saudi Arabia, and others as heretical. These essentials of belief are shared by the four classic schools of law: *Hanbali, Hanafi, Maliki,* and *Shafi.*

The modality of Islam which prevails in Saudi Arabia is a blend of the *Salafiyya* movement of Muhammad Abduh and the teachings of Muhammad ibn Abdul Wahhab. The official view in Saudi Arabia is that neither the term *Salafiyya* nor the term

Wahhabi is accurate. The belief that the creed of Saudi Arabia is simply Islam in its purest form is premised on several factors. First is the historical fact that it is the birthplace of the Prophet, the site where he received the Qur'an and where he lived, preached and is buried. Second is the absence of a complex, institutionalized religious system existing prior to Islam. Pre-Islamic Arabia was, relatively, a *tabula rasa*, hence the Islam which emerged was not seriously conditioned or modified by a competing system. Lastly, there was virtually no colonial influence in Saudi Arabia. The rule of the Ottomans in the Hejaz was Muslim rule and the influence of Aramco in Al-Hasa had no effect on Islam. The encrustations of Ottoman Islam were expunged by the purifying movement of Sheikh Muhammad ibn Abdul Wahhab in the 1740's. The relative pristinity of Islam in Saudi Arabia becomes evident upon comparison with Islamic behavior elsewhere.

The two most powerful modifying influences on Muslim societies have been colonial rule and pre-existing cultures. By its very existence the superordinate-subordinate relationship of colonialism eroded confidence in Islamic culture. Imperial hubris elevated values of the metropolitan powers. In some realms, particularly the French, to a lesser degree the British, Dutch and Italian, the consequent dialectic came perilously close to the substitution of one culture for another. French rule in North Africa and the Levant has produced a blend of French and Arab culture unique to the area. In architecture, ambience and social customs, for example, Lebanon, especially Beirut, was more French than Islamic. The introduction of grape cultivation and the manufacture of wine in North Africa is a symbol of this departure from orthodox Islamic teaching. In Turkey secularization was due not to the influence of an occupying colonial power but to the emulation of European culture by the charismatic influence of Kemal Ataturk. In India and Indonesia, Islamic behavior was affected by a powerful Hindu culture. In India and Pakistan today one finds *fakirs*, *pirs*, veneration of saints and graves which are proscribed in Saudi Arabia. There is a mystic quality derived perhaps from Sufism, Hinduism and pre-Islamic Zoroastrianism of Persia which colors behavior of village Islam sufficiently to justify a classification which some analysts have called "Indic Islam". In Indonesia the mysticism residing in the rich Hindu art, drama, and music of Java have profoundly influenced Islam.[70] The rise of Shiism to be the state religion in Iran may well have been influenced by pre-Islamic Persia. The inclination to strong monarchy in the form of kingship and in the power of the *imam* and the *ayatollah*, the sense of hierarchy, the love of regal splendor and panoply had all been glorified in the Persia of Cyrus.[71] Indeed the receptivity of Persia to Shiite Islam may have been conditioned by these very factors in ancient Persia. Peter J. Chelkowski and Ehsan Yarshater suggest that the elaborate veneration of Hussein and the theme of redemption through sacrifice and self-immolation had parallels in ancient Persia.[72]

Egypt has had a mixed cultural colonial legacy as complex as that of Iran. The Islamic domination, starting with the 7th century A.D., grafted politico-religious authoritarianism on ancient Pharaonic culture which had the same emphasis. The twelve year period of Napoleonic rule (1789-1801) encouraged a sense of nationalism and introduced elements of French law and bureaucratic organization. During the next period of rule under Mohammed Ali, large numbers of foreigners were brought in from Britain, France and Turkey to

provide technical assistance. When the British as-
sumed control in 1882 until Egyptian independence in
1922, there was massive infusion of British norms and
institutions of government. Much of what was introduced came by way of India where the British already
had long experience in colonial rule. We thus see in
Egypt one of the world's oldest civilizations and one
with clearly defined boundaries dating back in millen-
nia. On this Pharaonic culture of great sophistication
and grandeur, Islamic, French, British and now,
American, influences are grafted. The consequence is a
behavior unique to Egypt: somewhat secular and
westward-leaning but a bastion of Islamicity nonethe-
less. This is evidenced in the presence of Al-Azhar,
one of the world's oldest universities and regarded by
many as the global center of Islamic scholarship. This
cultural duality is also manifest by the existence of an
uncommonly robust Islamic militancy seriously chal-
lenging government and political stability.

Sectarian divisions in Islam are neither as pro-
nounced or as numerous as those in Christianity. The
1995 *World Almanac* lists 167 Christian denomina-
tions in the United States alone. Baptists appear to be
the most fractious, with 21 distinct persuasions. The
doctrinal differences within Christianity are profound.
These range from the orthodox literal interpretation of
scripture to belief in scripture as metaphor and myth.
The spectrum includes trinitarianism and unitarian-
ism, the liturgies embrace the sumptuous, ornate
splendors of the Orthodox and Catholic traditions as
well as the simplicity of the Quakers and Moravians.
And within the Christian embrace lie the doctrines
and practices of Christian Science and the Church of
Jesus Christ of Latter Day Saints.

When we compare the fact that Islam embraces no
deviation from its quintessentials with the divisions

in Christianity, it is misleading to use the term "sect" (which describes Christian divisions) to characterize Muslim differences. The term "modalities" in the Islamic context seems more appropriate.

The major division is that of the Sunni and Shia with the Sunni claiming about 85 percent. Shiism, the state religion of Iran also claims about 30 percent of the population of Pakistan. Nearly half the population of Iraq is Shia although the regime of Saddam Hussein is Sunni. The Alawi, a branch of the Shia, is the ruling elite under Hafiz al-Asad in Syria; the Shiites are a significant minority in Lebanon and a small minority (about 200 thousand) on the east coast of Saudi Arabia. The principal difference between these two modalities lies in the role of the religious leaders, *imams*, and especially the position of the *ayatollah*. This is linked to the notion of occultation, i.e. that certain *imams* have gone into hiding and may reappear at critical moments. This is a mystical aspect of Shiism which is rejected by the Sunni. Shiism emerged in about 632 A.D. from disagreement about leadership in Islam after the death of the Prophet. The dominant belief was that the leadership should be elected by the followers of the Prophet; this group became known as Sunni. Others, who felt that the leadership should pass by inheritance to Ali, the son-in-law of Muhammed and thence to his sons Hassan and Hussein, became known as Shiites. The defining moment came with the brutal assassination of Hussein in 680 A.D. in Kerbala (in modern Iraq). This event is commemorated with great fervor in Shiite communities with processions, self-flagellation and religious plays depicting the assassination.

Shiism is divided into several branches including the Alawites, the Zaidis (mostly in Yemen) and the Kharajites (in some parts of North Africa). The Ismaeli Shiites, scattered throughout the world, and headed by their *imam* Prince Karim Khan whose headquarters is in Geneva, concentrate on philanthropy for social causes. They deplore the emphasis in much of Islam on scriptural exegetics. They have given much developmental aid to social enterprises in remote areas and have established a Medical Center and College in Karachi which has become one of the most modern medical facilities in the Middle East. They do not typically enter politics or government service, hence are not a disruptive force in Muslim societies.

It is the Shia regime of Iran with its hegemonic impulse in Central Asia and Lebanon and its growing military and nuclear capability which is of concern to other Muslim regimes as well as to some Western countries. Where once the Shiites were regarded with disdain and even condescension by Sunnis, they are now viewed with apprehension, even fear, particularly in the Gulf states. These feelings have little to do with Islamic doctrine; like the origins of Shiism centuries ago, they have everything to do with power politics.

Another variation in modality is a group known as the Ahmadiyyas (also called Mirzai and Qadiani) named for their founder Mirza Ghulam Ahmad and for his abode--the village of Qadian in India. This group flourished in Pakistan but was declared "non-Muslim" by the National Assembly in 1974 because it violated the "Seal of the Prophet" by professing that its founder was a prophet following Mohammed. Ironically, the Ahmadiyyas have been zealous missionaries, especially in Africa and have been staunch practitioners of Islam wherever they have settled.

Cutting across these modalities, although found mostly among the Sunnis, is a tradition of Islamic mysticism called Sufism. The Sufis seek, either through asceticism or ecstatic experience such as dance, song or meditation, a direct communion with God. Sufis, found throughout the Muslim world, are a significant influence in Islam.

In addition to these modalities, several schools of law emerged during the two centuries after Muhammed's death in 633 A.D. The four most prominent schools, named for their founders who were influential scholars of Islam are followed today. These schools, mentioned earlier, differ with respect to the degree of reliance on *hadith*, on the reliability of *hadith*, and emphasis on consensus or on reason and analogy interpreting the Qur'an. Differences in the law of inheritance and marriage requirements have also emerged through the years. There is no deviation from the quintessentials of the faith. A Muslim may follow any school or all schools of law. Saudi Arabia recognizes the validity of all four schools in its *Shari'a* courts.

Another powerful and persuasive indicator of the complexity of the Muslim world and the force of culture as a modifier of behavior is ethnographic and linguistic diversity. Arabic is the language of the Qur'an; although it is translated into all major languages. Prayers are often recited in Arabic by non-Arabic speaking Muslims but Arabic is not the language of common use beyond the 22 Arab states or Arab communities in other states. Hundreds of other languages are spoken by Muslims: Persian, Urdu, Malayan, Swahili, Bengali, Turkish, Berber, to name but a few. These languages are derived from several different linguistic families and have different (though sometimes related) scripts. Strenuous efforts have been made to teach Arabic in all Muslim configurations, but it cannot be said that it is anywhere near universal in use.

Richard V. Weekes identifies some 300 distinct ethnic groups wholly or partly Muslim. He describes in detail 96 such groups whose Muslim populations exceed 100,000.[73] These 96 groups include more than 92 percent of the world's Muslims. These groups are not necessarily internal religious minorities, but are distinctive ethnic communities, sometimes speaking a different language from the majority in the country where they live. Often their domicile goes beyond national boundaries.

To illustrate the enormous cultural diversity of these ethnic groups, I have selected four: Berbers, Kurds, Tatars, Kashmiris, each of contemporary geopolitical importance. Each group reveals markedly different political and cultural configurations. Finally I describe briefly the five ethnic groups within Pakistan, a Muslim nation-state perennially agitated by ethno-linguistic differences.

Among the largest and most distinctive of such groups are the Berbers of North Africa, concentrated mainly in Morocco (34 percent of the population), Algeria (22 percent), Libya (5 percent), and Tunisia (3 percent). The Berbers' pre-Islamic veneration of saints has modified their contemporary practices. Some of their religious leaders (*marabouts*) are thought to have supernatural powers and are accorded the same saintly veneration.

Another such group are the Kurds living mainly in Turkey (10 million), Iran (5 million), Iraq (3.5 million), and Syria (1 million). Armenia and Azerbaijan each have about 10 thousand Kurds. There is also an indeterminate number, probably a 100 thousand, in the Russian Federation. Most of the Kurds are Sunni, although in Iran and parts of Iraq there are Shia minorities. Of all the Muslim ethnic groups, the Kurds are the most deserving of a separate homeland.[74]

Revolts to establish autonomy in Iran, Iraq and Turkey have not been successful. The Kurds' hopes raised by the Gulf War which they thought would establish an autonomous Kurdistan did not materialize. Instead, a zone north of the 36th parallel was established in Iraq, with U.N. forces protecting that zone from Iraqi incursions. Turkish pursuit of the PKK, a Kurdish guerrilla faction, across the Iraqi border in April 1995 suggests the complexity of the problem. The Kurds continue to press for autonomy, but because this would mean transfer of territory from all four countries (Iran, Iraq, Syria and Turkey) to create Kurdistan this does not seem likely in the foreseeable future.

The Tatars are noteworthy here because of their new relationship with the Russian Federation established by treaty in 1994 defining their status as one of 21 autonomous republics in the Federation.[75] The Republic of Tatarstan flies its own flag, elects it own president and enjoys a large measure of autonomy just short of national sovereignty. Descendants of the Tatar-Mongols of Manchuria, some 6 million Muslim Tatars are scattered throughout the former Soviet Union. Of the 3.7 million people in Tatarstan, Muslim Tatars only slightly outnumber ethnic Russians. Unlike other Muslim enclaves, Tatar Muslims have intermarried extensively with ethnic Russians and other non-Muslims. Their orthodoxy and fidelity to traditional Muslim behavior is somewhat more relaxed than found elsewhere. In the past several years, there has been an Islamic revival manifest in the restoration or construction of mosques and distribution of copies of the Qur'an. Tatarstan, one of the most highly developed republics in the Russian Federation, has a level of industrialization which compares favorably with industrialized parts of Russia. One of the reasons Russia has crushed the independence move-

ment of Chechnya, another Muslim autonomous republic, is the fear that Tatarstan might follow
Chechnya's example. To lose Tatarstan, in the heart of
Russia and only 400 miles east of Moscow, would be
more serious than losing Chechnya, on the southern
edge of Russia in the Caucasus. While Tatarstan has
protested Russia's action in Chechnya, there is little
sentiment to secede from the Federation.

The case of Kashmir is even more complex. Kashmiris are a distinctive ethnic group, largely Sunni,
with a long history of independence until the British
sold the territory to a Hindu Dogra chieftain, Gulab
Singh. Though subdivided by topography into
enclaves, some Buddhist and Hindu, the area was predominantly Muslim. Under British rule it became a
princely state, ruled by a Hindu maharajah, but usually
with a Muslim prime minister. On August 15, 1947,
when the Indian subcontinent was partitioned into independent India and Pakistan, Kashmir delayed in de-
ciding to join either. Under terms of the Radcliffe
Boundary Settlement, Kashmir would have normally
acceded to Pakistan since its population was 76 percent
Muslim and it was contiguous to Pakistan. During a
two-month period of indecision, an incursion of
Pakistani freedom fighters into Kashmir led the
Maharajah to ask India's help in repelling this force.
India refused until the Maharajah agreed to accede to
India. The Instrument of Accession was signed October
26, 1947 and the Indian army and air force entered the
conflict. Pakistani forces were pushed north to roughly
the 35th parallel, leaving two thirds of Kashmir,
including the Vale, Ladakh and Jammu under Indian
control. Hostilities continued until a ceasefire was
arranged by the United Nations, whose observers are
still stationed along the ceasefire line. A plebiscite, to
which India and Pakistan agreed, would undoubtedly

have resulted in accession to Pakistan. India refused to hold the plebiscite until Pakistan withdrew its forces from the northern one-third. Pakistan refused to do so and established a separate state of Azad Kashmir, closely linked to Islamabad. Since then, three wars between India and Pakistan have been fought. India is adamant in the view that Kashmir is an integral part of India and considers the matter closed. Some 1.5 million Kashmiri refugees are in Pakistan and nearly half a million are scattered throughout the world. The flight of Muslims and the in-migration of Hindus has changed the demographic composition somewhat. The latest census lists some 65 percent Muslim as compared with the 76 percent of 1947. Tens of thousands of Kashmiris have been killed as the Indian army has tightened its grip on the area. No resolution is in sight.[76]

Pakistan is the outstanding example of a nation-state embracing five distinct major ethnic groups and hundreds of sub-groups. These groups are Punjabi, Pathan, Sindhi, Baluchi and Muhajir (Urdu-speaking refugees from India). A sixth major group, Bengali, separated from Pakistan in 1971, creating the new Muslim state of Bangladesh. Each of these groups has its own language, literature, lifestyle and way of dress. The Pathans of the Northwest Frontier are ethnic Afghans whose traditions and languages are closer to Afghanistan than to their eastern neighbor, the Punjab. Never completely subdued by the British, they remain today a distinctive entity part of which is governed by the Frontier Crimes Regulations and its *jirga* system of justice rather than by the British legal system found in the rest of Pakistan. The Baluchi of Baluchistan are also a frontier tribal people with their own language, Brahui, and customs closer to the Baluchi of Iran and the Pathans than to the Punjabis.

In the southern province of Sindh, the ethnic problem is aggravated by the presence of thousands of refugees from India who speak Urdu rather than Sindhi. The resentment of the two groups for each other has led to political upheaval, and near anarchy, from which there seems to be no escape. The most serious ethnic trauma was the long-festering resentment of the Bengalis of East Pakistan, whose culture, climate, geography and personal temperament were more closely akin to Southeast Asia rather than to West Pakistan. The language differential was especially critical. Bengali is an ancient language with a written form derivative from Sanskrit. Its literature, especially poetry, is rich and profound. The dominant language of West Pakistan is Urdu whose script is a combination of Persian and Arabic. The Punjabi, Sindhi, Brahui and Pushtu vernaculars share this same base. The case of Pakistan is especially significant because it marks the triumph of ethnicity over religion. Not even Islam and the latent force of *ummah* could keep Pakistan united. The separation of the Bengalis may also be prelude to further fragmentation of the remaining five ethnic communities.

Another factor influencing cultural behavioral patterns is the impact of the dominant culture on minority Muslims, particularly in Europe and North America. This has become a matter of serious concern to first generation Muslim immigrants who see their children and grandchildren subjected to values which Islam regards as evil: teenage pregnancy, sexual promiscuity, abortion, drug dependency, immodesty of dress, rejection of religious values, pornography. Organizations like the Islamic Society of North America, the World Muslim League and the European Muslim Council have taken vigorous measures to deal with this problem.

6. Internal Minorities

The perception of a monolithic Islamic community is further dimmed by the presence of non-Muslim minorities living in Muslim states. Islamic law is rich in its empathy for and protection of such minorities. Islam recognizes the special status of members of Judaism and Christianity as "People of the Book" (*ahl-al-kitab*): those who believe in the sacred status of the Old Testament Such persons (*dhimmis* or *kitabis*), for example, are allowed in a non-Muslim state to recite the authorized prayer at the *halal* slaughter of animals for food.[77] They are guaranteed the right to worship, to vote and to hold government positions. Exceptions can be made if such activities are inimical to the Muslim nature of the society. Under this rubric, some Muslim states restrict freedom of worship and the right of non-Muslims to hold office.

Christians are a numerically significant minority in Muslim states. It is estimated that in the Middle East alone there are some 12 million or 10 percent of the population. Lebanon, before the civil war, had a Christian population of nearly 40 percent of the total. Egypt has about 8 million Copts and Syria about one million Christians. About 10 percent of the Palestinian diaspora are Christian. Pakistan for many years had a devout Roman Catholic, A. R. Cornelius, as Chief Justice of the Supreme Court. Its Roman Catholic minority, largely of Goan ancestry, is led by Joseph Cardinal Cordeiro. The valuable properties of both the Catholic and the Anglican churches, although in some cases unused, have never been threatened with expropriation. Jordan also has a Christian community and its Foreign Minister, Dr. Kamal Abu Jaber, is a Christian. Iraq, which is about three percent Christian (largely Chaldean, Nestorian, Orthodox, Catholic and

Protestant) has a Chaldean Christian, Tariq Aziz, as Deputy Prime Minister. In Egypt, a Coptic Christian, Boutros Boutros Ghali, was Deputy Prime Minister prior to his appointment as United Nations Secretary General. Morocco has flourishing Jewish and Christian communities. Turkey, as an avowedly secular state with strong European leanings, is tolerant of its Christian minority. It is true that these minorities live in societies with an overwhelming Muslim ethos and are often not confident of their status as *dhimmis*. The traditions of Islamic law are their sole protection. To be sure, this tolerance is not practiced in all Muslim countries. Saudi Arabia does not allow separate buildings for worship by non-Muslims. The Bahais, a sect originating in Persia, have been banned in Muslim states as heretical. This is because they have violated a cardinal principle of Islam in their belief in a prophet after Muhammed. The radical states of Libya and the Sudan have experienced acts of violence against non-Muslims. Egypt has had difficulty controlling terrorist acts against Coptic Christians. Perhaps the principal advantage of the Christian minorities in Muslim states is their network of influence with Christians in the West. This makes for improved understanding of the Muslim condition and may moderate perceptions of the non-Muslim world.

Christian influence in the Middle East has been profound. The American University of Beirut established in 1866 as Protestant College and the Catholic (Jesuit) University of Saint Joseph established in Beirut in 1881 have trained much of the medical, scientific, political and intellectual leadership of the Middle East. Robert College in Istanbul has had similar, though lesser influence. The leadership elites trained at these institutions have not necessarily been Christian. On the contrary, most have been Muslim. Arab churches

in the Middle East have been influential bridges between Muslims and Christians. Frank Sakran, a representative of the Greek Orthodox (Arab) Church to the
World Council of Churches, has been particularly effective. In the United States Archbishop Philip E.
Saliba, Primate of the Antiochian Orthodox Christian
Church of North America, heads the influential
Standing Conference of Middle Eastern and Christian
leaders. Libya's Muammar al-Qadafi, not usually por-
trayed in the American press as a conciliatory figure,
has spoken and acted in behalf of Muslim-Christian
understanding.

7. Differences in Polity

The 52 Islamic nations, though bonded in the metaphysical realm by common religious belief, are widely
separated by differences in state polity. Those differences have been induced or aggravated by colonial rule
and by post-colonial enmeshment in a web of new imperialism now cultural and economic. Weak or embryonic political structures cannot easily sustain a
polity which is truly indigenous and in harmony with
its own cultural and historical circumstances when it is
subjected to the transnational commercial and cultural
dynamism of the United States, a radiating power of
enormous energy and hubris.[78] Nor is robust resistance
possible when the web of dependency is spun with
threads of gold poised to break unless externally for-
mulated standards of political structure and behavior
are met. The greater the integration of Muslim polities
with the world at large, the greater the dependence on
technologically advanced systems and the greater the
threat to distinctive indigenous religious and cultural
values. Differing political systems are also the consequences of varying perceptions of the nature of an

Islamic state and often of amateurish flirtation with Western political concepts and structures. These include single party and multi-party systems, parliamentary and presidential patterns, unicameral and bicameral legislatures, judicial review, socialism, communism, capitalism, and free vs. controlled market economies. Even such flirtatious experiments cannot be independent for they are enmeshed in the web of political systems left by colonial rule. That web is too tightly woven to permit escape. The result is a veritable kaleidoscopic display of governmental systems. A few examples of the variations are illustrative.

Pakistan, subjected to the triple trauma of two centuries of British rule, separation from India, and the secession of East Pakistan (to become Bangladesh) is an extreme case. It had four constitutions, thus rearranging the crucial relationship of space, power and culture four times. It had two periods of martial law and massive infusion of American technical assistance. Two heroic efforts were made to escape the web of dependence on the West. The first was the decade (1958-1969) old experiment in Basic Democracies initiated during the regime of Ayub Khan. The second was the ten-year (1977-1988) political structure, *Nizam-i-Mustafa* (Way of the Prophet) evolved in the regime of Zia ul-Haq. Both were courageous and brilliant efforts to throw off colonial and post-colonial intervention and establish an indigenous polity. The Basic Democracies scheme attracted favorable world-wide attention and had it continued longer it might well have been a model for other developing countries. The fall of the government of Ayub Khan and his replacement first by Yayha Khan then by Zulfikar Ali Bhutto and the distraction of the secession of East Pakistan brought about the demise of this notable experiment. *Nizam-i-Mustafa* was a different scheme which sought to evolve an Islamic polity through serious efforts to revise the legal system in accordance with Shari'a. While this was popular with such groups as the *Jamaat-i-Islami*, it was resisted by others of a more secular persuasion. In any event *Nizam-i-Mustafa* collapsed with the death of Zia ul-Haq in a mysterious airplane crash in 1988 in which the United States ambassador Arnold Raphel, was also killed. The successor governments of Benazir Bhutto and Nawaz Sharif had no interest in the creation of their predecessor. The faltering remnant of the parliamentary system introduced under British colonial rule has proved incapable of coping effectively with the horrendous problems of refugees and bitter regional feuds.

Saudi Arabia is at the other end of the spectrum of comparison. Its religious, linguistic and ethnic cohesion is unmatched. It did not experience colonial rule, hence did not suffer from a disarticulation created by the forced imposition of foreign norms and institutions. In the context of comfortable wealth it constructed its own polity with the Qur'an as its constitution. It did not have to struggle to reconcile British or French law with Islamic law. It functioned under Islamic law (*shari'a*), selectively integrating extraneous elements to meet new needs. It built institutions before it expanded political participation and then gradually evolved an appointed representative system (*Majlis al-Shoura*) in 1993. The Saudi polity cannot be fitted into Western categories. Neither an absolute monarchy nor a constitutional monarchy of British pattern, it is as nearly indigenous as can be found.

Iran's polity has a similar indigenous quality, achieved by a different course. The first difference is its history of imperial greatness dating back to Cyrus and Darius in the 6th century B.C. There followed waves of Greek, Parthian, Roman and Arab conquest. By 650

A.D. the Sassanid empire fell to the Arabs and indigenous Zoroastrianism was replaced by Islam. A long period of Muslim dynasties evolved into constitutional government in the early 20th century. There then followed a period of monarchical rule under Reza Shah and his successor, Pahlavi Shah. Throughout much of this history the idea of monarchy and intense feelings of devotion to Shia Islam were dominant. In the twentieth century, until 1979, the cultural influence of the West, especially France, Britain and the United States was important. The Khomeini revolution was a drastic effort to establish an indigenous polity. It almost totally detached that polity from the ideological premises and economic and political structures of the international state system of the West. By emphasizing its predominantly non-Arab ethnicity and its Shiite Islam, it has distanced itself somewhat from the ideology and transactions of the Islamic *ummah*. Its development in the twentieth century has been marked also by its relative wealth rather than abject poverty. Like Saudi Arabia, Iran has thus developed an Islamic system of government. Unlike the futile efforts in Pakistan, it has done so by disengaging from a long, rich and complicated past of foreign influence. But its tactic was revolution rather than gradualism and thus far it has successfully forged a relatively indigenous political system.

The Indonesian case is characterized by the penetrating influence of Hinduism. Western constitutional government, learned from Dutch colonial rule, did not penetrate as deeply as British tutelage in India. There was no imperial past as in Iran, nor an indigenous Islamicity as in Saudi Arabia. Islam was dominant since the 14th century, but was not exclusive, Hinduism still prevailed in many parts. The postcolonial period, starting with 1948 under Sukarno and continued under Soharto, has been dominated by a unique brand of secularism tinged with Islam. The ideology of *Pancasila* is the national civic religion and is part of the 1945 constitution under which Indonesia is ruled. The five principles of *Pancasila*, nationalism, humanity (internationalism), consultation (democracy), social justice, and belief in a Supreme Being, effectively separate the secular and the sacerdotal, an equation difficult for Muslims to accept. By making adjustments in the applicability of Islam in family law, the pluralistic, secular structure has endured and Islam, while not enjoying cultural exclusivity, continues to exist as the religion of 90 percent of the population.

Other mutations in forms of government in Muslim states, while not as striking as the examples given above, are equally revealing. Morocco and Jordan have variations of constitutional monarchy. Libya's Muammar al-Qadafi has invented an "Islamic Arabic Socialist Mass-State". Syria and Iraq live in the somewhat distorted shadows of discarded monarchy created by the British and the indigenous socialist ideology of Michel Aflaq. The Baathist legacy of Aflaq has taken a different turn in each but a brutal dictatorship of a Sunni minority (Iraq) and a Shia/Alawite minority (Syria) characterizes both. Malaysia, with a slight majority Muslim population and a long history of British rule, has evolved its own form of government based on a blend of kingship and parliamentary government. Each state has its own sultan. The sultans become head (*Yang di-Pertuan Agong*) of Malaysia for fixed terms in order of seniority. There is a strong party system and elections to parliament. Under the prime ministership of Dr. Mahathir, the Islamic nature of society is given prominence, but under different, less intensely Muslim leadership, Islam would have a less dominant role.

In the struggle to relate Islam to a polity Muslim states must cope with pre-Islamic indigenous heritage, experience of colonial rule, international influences on the economy and culture, indigenous Islamic forces, and relations with the Muslim *ummah*. There is no common agreement among them as to what constitutes an Islamic state.

8. Religious Complementarities

The relationship of the three monotheistic Abrahamic religions, Judaism, Christianity and Islam, is not necessarily one of mutual antagonism. Certainly the theological connections are evident and have been analyzed in an enormous volume of literature. Earlier parts of this essay described Islam's special consideration of *ahl al-kitab*, people of the book: Jews and Christians. All three religions share a common respect, even reverence, for Old Testament prophets. The naming of Muslims for the Prophets should not go unnoticed, though it may be obscured by Arabization. Moses becomes Musa; Abraham: Ibrahim; Solomon: Sulyman; Mary: Maryam; David: Daoud; Jesus: Issa; John: Yayha; Joseph: Yusif, to name but a few. The complementarities with Christianity include belief in the virgin birth of Christ, though not in the resurrection, crucifixion, ascension, nor in the Trinity or divinity of Christ. Muslims are attentive to if not celebratory of Christmas. Prince Bandar, the current Saudi ambassador to the United States, sends Christmas cards in Arabic with an English translation of part of *Sura* (chapter) 3 of the Qur'an called *Al-i-Imran sura* which describes the angel's announcement to Mary of the coming virgin birth of Christ. Perhaps the best way to demonstrate both the adherence to this belief and to the sanctified literalism of the Qur'an is to relate the experience of the American Unitarian clergyman, Moncure D. Conway. In 1905 Conway met in Calcutta with a group of "Brahmans, Brahmos, Moslems and Parsis" to discuss religious and philosophical subjects. One of the Brahmans asked his opinion about the "miraculous birth of Christ." Conway responded that he regarded it like the legend of the virgin-born deity of the Hooghly River, "....a story of mythological and poetic interest but not to be regarded as historical." The Brahman said that was also his opinion of both events. Conway then continues to relate this revealing exchange: "The Moslems, of whom there were a dozen of high rank in the room, had said nothing and I remarked that I would like to hear their opinion. Thereupon the Moslems bent their richly turbaned heads together in private consultation. At length one of them arose and said that they all felt 'bound to accept the narrative just as it stands in the New Testament.'" Conway concluded that "the Moslems were the only orthodox Christians present." Elsewhere in his study of religions Conway had found the same views. In Colombo he had concluded that the "Moslems are not Christians, but the only ones in the East who maintain literally all of the miracles ascribed to Christ in the gospels or related to his birth. It is very rare to find among them a sceptic."[79]

This view of the Qur'an and hence the historicity of Christ's birth is as prevalent today as it was in Conway's time. This can be illustrated by an event in England in 1993. A British television series, *Spitting Image*, featured a rubber puppet of Jesus styled as a hippie. The Ahmadiyya Muslim Association protested, pointing out that Muslims revere Jesus and that those responsible for the television series should be severely punished. The puppet was withdrawn. The producer said that he had discussed the puppet with Church of England leaders who regarded it as "innocuous." The Muslims' committee said that the Anglican clergy "should be heartened by the leadership provided by British Muslims in protesting [Christian] blasphemy."[80]

The only predominantly Muslim country in Europe is the newly independent, tragically beleaguered nation of Bosnia-Herzegovina. The brutal massacre of Muslim Bosnians by Orthodox Christian Serbs serves as a chilling backdrop for the projection of Muslim-Christian relations. Yet the Muslim Bosnian President, Alija Ali Izetbegovic, wrote prophetically that kinship between Islam and Christianity has been overlooked. "Their kinship, if we draw all the necessary conclusions from it, could direct the relations of these two great world religions to an entirely new dimension in the future. ... As Islam in the past was the intermediary between the ancient cultures and the West, it must again today, in a time of dramatic dilemmas and alternatives, shoulder its role as intermediary nation in a divided world. This is the meaning of the third way, the Islamic way."[81]

The importance of this kinship is reflected in the establishment of new academic structures. Among them is the Centre for the Study of Islam and Christian-Muslim Relations at Selly Oak College in Birmingham, England. The Centre publishes *Islam and Christian-Muslim Relations* semi-annually. In the United States, Georgetown University established the Center for Muslim-Christian Understanding in 1993.

Relations between Jews and Muslims have not always been hostile. There were times in Islamic history, especially during Muslim ascendancy in Spain (711-1212 A.D.) when Jews were well treated and often sought Muslim sanctuary from Christian persecution.

The Jewish historian, Mark Cohen, asserts that Jews fared better in the Muslim world and challenges the "countermyth of Islamic persecution" that has prevailed since the Six-Day War of 1967.[82] The sentiment of Muslim states towards Jews is a political statement about Zionism, the establishment of Israel, the displacement of Palestinians, control of Jerusalem and the third holiest site in Islam: *Al Quds al-Haram* (the Dome of the Rock). Inevitably this political sentiment, brewing for half a century, translates into attitudes towards Jews as people. But historically this has not been the root cause. It is conceivable that with the achievement of a just Middle East peace settlement, Jewish-Muslim relations will improve and that the constantly invoked theme of "Judaeo-Christian" tradition will be expanded to "Judaeo-Christian-Islamic".

The values and ethical systems of these three Abrahamic monotheisms are quintessentially compatible despite some theological differences and varying interpretations of scripture and history. In the face of what appears to be the disintegration of Western civilization, comparable, the apocalyptics tell us, to the fall of Rome, a unified front of all other-worldly perspectives is needed. The start has been made in Jewish-Christian and Christian-Muslim relations. Now the urgent need is for a similar Jewish-Muslim reconciliation.

VII

CONSPECTUS

The one billion people who profess Islam are not concentrated in a single, unbroken land mass. This differs from the one billion Chinese or the near-billion concentration of population on the subcontinent of India. Any imagery of a great green horde, controlled by a single government, capable of raising enormous land armies, is fallacious. The major divisions of the world's Muslim population can roughly be divided in this way: 220 million Arabs live in 22 Arab states (members of the League of Arab States) (*dar al-Islam*); 450 million Muslims live in some 33 non-Arab but Muslim states (members of the Organization of the Islamic Conference (*dar al-Islam*); 330 million live as minorities in every non-Muslim nation in the world (*dar al-harb*); 20 million (a rapidly fluctuating number) refugees are scattered in a global diaspora often displaced within their homelands (*dar al-muhajirin*).

The overwhelming majority of Muslims live in abject poverty. The 1994 per capita Gross Domestic Product (GDPpc in U.S. dollars) of the countries in which they live range from the lowest--Mozambique (115), Sudan (184), Chad (190), Afghanistan (200), Bangladesh (200) to the highest--Qatar (17,000), United Arab Emirates (13,800), Kuwait (11,000), Brunei (8,800), Bahrain (7,800), Saudi Arabia (6,500). Nor do minorities necessarily live in countries of better economic circumstances. India, which has the world's largest Muslim minority, has a GDPpc of 270; China's is 360. Minorities in western industrialized countries are better off, a fact which partly accounts for Muslim migration to those countries. The outstanding example is the Algerian influx to France. These GDPpc figures have meaning when compared to those of such industrialized western countries as France (18,900), Germany (17,400), United Kingdom (15,900), and Canada (19,600).

The poverty of Muslim nations is aggravated by high rates of natural population increase. Iraq, Libya and Syria have a natural increase of 3.7 percent--the highest rates in the world. They are closely followed by Niger, Pakistan, Libya, Jordan and Iran with rates from 3.0 to 3.7 percent. Morocco and Algeria, whose population increases are a source of concern to France, rank next with percentages of 2.2 and 2.3 respectively. These figures are alarming when compared with those for other non-industrial states such as India (1.6 percent) and China (1.1) and with industrial states such as Japan (0.3), Italy (0.1), France (0.4), United Kingdom (0.3) and the United States (0.7). The global Muslim population is expanding much more rapidly than non-Muslims. This is likely to increase religious and ethnic tensions and to enhance the prospect of Islamic-non-Islamic confrontation. This is all the more reason for strenuous efforts towards mutual understanding and accommodation.

Muslims live in a kaleidoscopic array of political systems ranging from the secular republican polity of Turkey to the Islamic constitutional systems of Iran and Saudi Arabia. The character of the *ummah* is essentially spiritual; it owes no allegiance to nation-states; it transcends them. Yet in the real world the nation-state is the dominant political authority and the *ummah* is realized mainly in rhetoric and in a slowly emerging pattern of pan-Islamic structures which will probably grow in importance. Islamic unity is weakened by significant divisions, especially by those created by the hegemonic impulse of a secular-leaning Iraq and similar impulses of an Islamic-oriented Iran. The violent acts committed by a variety of groups from different nations, some claiming an Islamic identity, and others having that identity conferred on them by the West, have been consistently condemned by Muslim states and Muslim international organizations. There are sporadic upsurges of Islamic militancy but they should not be regarded as a globally-planned movement embracing the whole Muslim world.

The dangers which the apocalyptic forecasters tell of the "Green Menace" are not, then, dangers of a global uprising against the West. The threat lies in the possible control of Egypt, Algeria, the Sudan and Saudi Arabia by militant Muslim absolutists who, linked with Iran and Iraq, may not hesitate to use violence. Their first line of attack would be seizure of internal power.

The dilemma lies in dissatisfaction of populations with regimes which are perceived as corrupt and even un-Islamic. When groups such as the National Salvation Front of Algeria are denied their share of duly elected power by invalidation of the election by a military regime, this may generate violence. When the invalidation is supported by foreign powers, the discontent becomes internationalized and external violence is perceived as justified protection against foreign intervention.

The proper role for the West is not to interfere in the play of internal political forces in a sovereign state. Mature, western political systems can deal with regimes even though power is held by agents deemed antagonistic. When such regimes act externally by aggression (as in the case of Iraq) or by proven complicity in international acts of violence, the intervention may be justified.

The Confucian-Islamic connection described by Huntington is not out of the question. But it presupposes a Pakistan allied with the Islamic absolutists and a China and North Korea actively embarked on international mischief. It also presupposes a western world blind to Muslim fears and aspirations. Western failure to act in Kashmir, Chechnya, Bosnia, and reluctance initially to act in Afghanistan, and its distorted inequitable participation in the Palestinian question, lends credibility to this assumption. That presupposition could be corrected; all these conditions are reversible.

The problems faced internally by the Muslim world appear to be overwhelming. Muslims perceive their values to be increasingly dissonant from those of western liberalism which seems to have lost its moorings in piety, morality and ethics. Islamic polities must be perceived as part of a total epistemology, hence must be judged by their own internally-generated criteria. Yet the criteria are subjected to internal conflict as to their meaning and their relationship to the non-Muslim world.

Every great issue of human existence: liberty, justice, welfare, security, dignity, respect, enlightenment, rectitude, death, affection, divine will and divine message has its own scriptural inspiration and internal consistency. It is especially difficult for the West to understand the tacit, indwelling nature of the Muslim psyche. There is no agreed-upon technique for analyzing the salience of the non-verbal, intuitive dimension of man's being: a dimension which forms an important part of Muslim identity. Only when Spengler's metaphor of the "world cavern" and his use of the term "soul" are understood can the perennial dialectic of the *ummah* and the modern nation-state have meaning.

Perhaps the greatest challenge is the alternately harmonious and abrasive confrontation of the Islamic and non-Islamic worlds. The Muslim value system is an all-embracing, all-encompassing moral and aesthetic continuum. Yet it is not iconoclastic or exclusive. On the contrary, its dominion is universal and it is unfettered as to time, space or race. The coherence and integrity of its own belief system must be self-maintaining and yet be used as a radiating source for its universalization. This must be achieved within the context of a world order predominantly non-Islamic and which places the Muslim world in a position of dependency. Such a subordination is acerbated by the juggernaut of non-Muslim cultural and commercial imperialism propelled by a dynamic of communications technology and entrepreneurial hubris.

The Muslim world must preserve its values, reconcile conflicting values, yet achieve that reconciliation without overt hostile confrontation with non-believers. Important strides have been taken at the ideological level with Christianity; the next step should be with Judaism. The internal mechanism for achieving all reconciliations is well ensconced in Islamic doctrine: *ijtihad*. The problem is that of dislodging the mechanism from two threatening webs. The first is the violent minority element in Islamic society whose actions may justify the use of the term "rage" characterizing the work of Lewis, Wright, Worsethorne and others. The second is extricating the interpretations from the encrustations and iconoclasms of village exegesis (the *mullah* mentality) so that it can function in an enlightened way without betraying Qur'anic truths. Regrettably, these two threats are often united in the same person or group.

There is a significant movement, scattered geographically, to reinterpret Islam to fit the present age. This is consistent with *ijtihad*. Those bent on such reform are in Jordan, Egypt, Turkey, Algeria and Iran. They are typically professional people educated in the West. They do not repudiate Islam. On the contrary, they are devout observing Muslims in the tradition of Sir Mohammed Iqbal, the poet-philosopher of India whose *Reconstruction of Religious Thought in Islam* (1934) remains a classic. These reforms are opposed by traditionalist clerics and by radical militants, neither of whom favor the western style democracy which the reformers advocate.

A different reform effort is that labelled "Islamic literalist" which seeks to replace pro-western Islamic regimes with anti-western Islamic ideologies. These movements are attractive to young Muslims and may, in some analysts' view be the beginning rather than the end of "the militant Islamic movement".[83]

Although the non-Islamic world manifests an ecumenical interest in Islam as a religion, it is often based on issues of global political power and national security rather than on respect and esteem. There is some evidence, as this essay has pointed out, of a concurrent movement towards a true ideological comprehension arising from a base of religious complementarity and agreement on social issues.

Only a courageous assertion of the Muslim value system proclaimed by an authoritative global political structure can command the respect and esteem of that part of the world which repudiates Muslim values even while holding hands across the creeds. The present kaleidoscopic array of loose institutional segments in the Muslim world must be reassembled in a cohesive paradigm and structure which gives meaning and influence to the concept of *ummah*. This paradigm and structure must be capable both of capturing the imagination of the Muslim psyche and uniting the *ummah* spiritually if not politically. This condition appears to be slowly emerging. The evolution of intra-Islamic attention to minorities and refugees, more forceful assertion of Muslim values and political power and conciliatory gestures toward other faiths: these are glimmers of hope. Only the resolution of these issues will restore the world of Islam to the distinctive position of global influence commensurate with its territorial domain and its demographic strength.

In reasserting the paramountancy of its culture it must continue to disclaim all forms of violence. This has already been done by the Gulf Cooperation Council, the Organization of the Islamic Conference and by individual states. It must also reject the specious unilinear concept of "westernization". The Islamic world is an example of the circularity of culture change and of the permeability of civilizational boundaries. It has, after all, been one of the foremost sources for the radiation and reception of values, and the transmission and translation of values from one culture to another, in the history of the world. Probably no other civilization, neither Greek, Roman or Persian, has had global experience in all five processes radiation, receptivity, transmission, translation and preservation of culture change. Anyone fully cognizant of this aspect of Islamic development would immediately comprehend the views of Spengler, Toynbee, Northrop, Berdyaev, and Malinowski.

It is a cruel irony that at the moment when Islam is free of colonial domination and some of its segments are endowed with a degree of wealth, it is plagued and fragmented by intra-Islamic conflict, sporadic violence by minority groups and dependence upon the technetronic largesse of the non-Muslim world. A true recovery of Islamic identity cannot be achieved in the context of these three obstacles. Lebanon and the Palestinian problem must be stabiized and enmities between Muslim states must be sedated. Violent acts attributed to Muslim impulse must be seen as small percentages of such acts committed world-wide: 21 percent of the incidents and 31% of organizations with Middle East/Islam connections for the five-year period 1990-94. Muslim foreign policy must be coordinated, reconciliation or at least an understanding between Muslim and non-Muslim values must be achieved. The global Muslim political structures now in existence (such as LAS, OIC, GCC) must be strengthened.

The most optimistic hope for the Muslim world lies in the differentials in piety and dynamism which now exist between Islam and the non-Muslim world. The Muslim value system appears to be more pristine, more intact than the doctrines of Christianity which are increasingly being relegated to the realm of myth or fanaticism. In consequence, zeal and intensity of piety may be diminishing. Islam, on the other hand, is in a dynamic, effervescent stage of development. We cannot predict how long these conditions may last or whether they may be reversed, i.e. Islam in decline and non-Islam in the ascendancy. But at this moment in history the dynamics and clearly defined values of Islam have the potential for resuscitating the western world's decline to morbidity. This can be done only if the image projected by Islam on the global screen and the actions of Muslims on the world stage are compatible with Islamic principles of peace, justice, and reverence for life.

ENDNOTES

1. See, for example, Michael W. Suleiman, *The Arabs in the Mind of America* (Brattleboro, VT: Amana Books, 1988); Edward W. Said, *Covering Islam* (New York: Pantheon Books, 1981); Jack G. Shaheen, *The T.V. Arab* (Bowling Green, OH: Bowling Green State University Press, 1981); Janice J. Terry, *Mistaken Identity: Arab Stereotypes in Popular Writing* (Washington, D.C., American-Arab Affairs Council, 1985); Edward Ghareeb, *Split Vision: the Portrayal of Arabs in the American Media*, (Washington, D.C., American-Arab Affairs Council, 1983).

2. Leon Uris, *The Haj* (New York: Doubleday, 1984)

3. *New York Times*, July 14, 1993. See also the account by Michael Saba, *Arab News* (Riyadh) July 24, 1993.

4. Karl E. Meyer, "Woodmen and Desert Men", in "Editorial Notebook", *New York Times* January 29, 1990.

5. *Arab News* (Riyadh) November 25, 1994.

6. Michael Quinn, "Where Have You Gone, Omar Sharif?," *Time*, August 8, 1994, p. 19.

7. Yossef Bodansky, *Target America and the West* (New York: Shapolsky Publishers, 1993). See also Dr. Michael P. Saba "Muslim States Projected As New 'Evil Empire'" *Arab News* (Riyadh) April 2, 1992.

8. Peregrine Worsethorne "Islam: Exorcising the Western Gods. . ." reprinted from the London *Sunday Telegraph* in *The Wall Street Journal* January 25, 1979.

9. Amos Perlmutter, "Containment Strategy for the Islamic Holy War", *The Wall Street Journal*, October 4, 1984.

10. Bernard Lewis "The Roots of Muslim Rage", *The Atlantic Monthly* September, 1990, pp. 47-60. The extent of this article's influence is suggested by the fact that Samuel Huntington in his controversial piece "The Clash of Civilizaions?" cites the Lewis article as one of two sources supporting his own prognosis of the danger of Islam. See pp. 9-18 below, and notes 13, 15, 16 for analysis of Huntington's hypotheses. The ideological perspectives of Lewis are examined in considerable detail and with very little sympathy in Edward W. Said, *Orientalism* (New York: Pantheon Books, 1978) pp. 105, 107, 315-21, 332, 335-36, 343, 349-50.

11. Robin Wright, *Sacred Rage: The Wrath of Militant Islam* (New York: Linden Press, Simon and Schuster, 1985).

12. Reported by Paul Klebnikov in, "An Interview with Aleksandr Solzhenitsyn", *Forbes*, May 9, 1994, pp. 118-112.

13. Samuel P. Huntington, "The Clash of Civilizations?", *Foreign Affairs* Vol 72, No. 3 Summer 1993, pp. 22-49.

14. X, "Sources of Soviet Conduct", *Foreign Affairs*, Vol 25 July 1947, pp. 566-582.

15. "Comments", *Foreign Affairs*, Vol. 72, No. 4 September/October 1993, pp. 2-21. The commentators were Fouad Ajami, Majid Khadduri Professor of Middle Eastern Studies, School of Advanced International Studies, Johns Hopkins University; Kishore Mahbubani, Deputy Secretary of Foreign Affairs, Singapore: Robert L. Bartley, Editor of *The Wall Street Journal*; Lin Binyan, Director of the Princeton China Initiative; and Jeane J. Kirkpatrick, former U.S. Ambassador to the United Nations. Appended to those critiques were brief notes by Albert L. Weeks, Professor Emeritus of International Relations at New York University an Gerald Piel, Chairman Emeritus of *Scientific American Inc*.

16. Samuel P. Huntington, " If Not Civilizations, What?", *Foreign Affairs* Vol. 72, No. 5, November/December 1993, pp. 186-194.

17. See, for example, articles written in the *Arab News* (Ridayh) by: Abdul Wahab Bashir, December 12, 1994; Dr. Michael Saba, September 1, 1994; Dr. Abdul Qader Tash, November 10, 1993; Nicholas Doughty, August 11, 1994.

18. See, for example, Peter Steinfels, "Beliefs", *The New York Times*, April 16, 1994 and George Melloan, "Cultures in Conflict on the Global Battlefield", *The Wall Street Journal*, August 16, 1993. William Pfaff *International Herald Tribune*, November 4, 1993 and July 7, 1994; Stephen S. Rosenfeld, "Algeria Offers A Test of Civilization Theory", *The Washington Post*, June 25-26, 1994; Edward P. Djerejian, "A Five-Step Plan for Working With Islam", *The Christian Science Monitor*, March 17, 1995.

19. Robert D. Kaplan, "The Coming Anarchy", *The Atlantic Monthly*, February 1994, pp. 44-76, esp. pp. 62-63. Kaplan's principal reliance is on the global, demographic emphasis in Thomas Fraser Homer-Dixon "On the Threshold: Environmental Changes as Causes of Acute Conflict", *International Security*, Vol. 16, No. 2, 1991, pp. 76-116. For his analysis of Islam, his point of departure is Huntington's essay.

20. Zbigniew Brzezinski, *Out of Control* (New York: Scribners, 1993) p. 166 n.* See also p. 210

21. Richard Nixon, *Beyond Peace* (New York: Random House, 1994) pp. 153 ff.

22. Brian Beedham, "Islam and the West", *The Economist*, August 6th, 1994. pp. 3-18, esp. pp. 3-5. Kishore Mahbubani takes issue with Beedham's assumption that Islamic societies must become more western. Islam and Asian

societies will and should develop in their own unique ways. Kishore Mahbubani, "The Pacific Way", *Foreign Affairs*, Vol. 74, No. 1 January/February 1995, pp. 100-111. The basic argument of my essay sustain's Mahbubani's observation.

23. Oswald Spengler, *The Decline of the West* (New York: Alfred Knopf, 1926. rev. ed) esp. Vol. I, p. 32.

24. Nicolas Berdyaev, *The Meaning of History* (London: The Centenary Press 1936) See esp. pp. 207-224.

25. Arnold J. Toynbee, *A Study of History* Somervell Abridgement (London: Oxford University Press, 1946).

26. F.S.C. Northrop, *The Meeting of East and West* (New York: Macmillan, 1946). Quotation at p. 296. See also his *The Taming of the Nations* (New York: Macmillan, 1952).

27. Pitirim A. Sorokin, *Social Philosophies in an Age of Crisis* (Boston: The Beacon Press 1950). pp. 279 ff. See also his *Social and Cultural Dynamics* (Boston: Porter Sargent 1957).

28. F.R. Cowell, *History, Civilization and Culture* (Boston: The Beacon Press 1952), p. 9.

29. Bronislaw Malinowski, *The Dynamics of Culture Change* (New Haven, Yale University Press 1955). pp. 17-140.

30. Norman Daniel, *The Cultural Barrier: Problems in the Exchange of Ideas* (Edinburgh: Edinburgh University Press, 1975) pp. 13-14. I am indebted to Dr. Mona Abu-Fadl for calling my attention to this book. See also n. 26 above.

31. Ralph Braibanti, "The Relevance of Political Science to the Study of Underdeveloped Areas", in Ralph Braibanti and Joseph J. Spengler, eds, *Tradition, Values, and Socio-*

Economic Development (Durham, NC: Duke University Press, 1961.) pp. 139-180, esp. the schematic diagram on p. 154. See also Ralph Braibanti, "Political Development: Contextual, Non-Linear Perspectives", *Politikon*, No. 3, October, 1976, pp. 6-18.

32. As reported in Amir Taheri, "French Perceptions of Islam and Muslims", *Arab News* (Riyadh) December 12, 1993.

33. Jean Raspail, *The Camp of the Saints* (Petoskey, MI: The Social Contract Press, 1994).

34. In Matthew Connelly and Paul Kennedy, "Must it Be the Rest Against the West?", *The Atlantic Monthly*, December 1994, pp. 61-84, esp. p. 69.

35. As reported in *Arab News* (Riyadh) October 10, 1994. See also *The Wall Street Journal*, January 1, 1995.

36. Lamis Moufti, "The headscarfs issue in France: A lawyer's point of view", *Arab News*, (Riyadh) December 5, 1994. Lee Kuan Yew, former prime minister of Singapore and one of the most astute statesmen of our time deplores emphasizing cultural separativness in a nation. But he puts Muslims in "a slightly different category because they are extremely sensitive about their customs, especially diet". He would deal with the headdress problem by permitting it to be worn in school and by being "prepared to put up with the strangeness". Fareed Zakaria, "Culture is Destiny: A Conversation with Lee Kuan Yew", *Foreign Affairs*, Vol. 73, March/April 1994, p. 121.

37. As reported in *Arab News* (Riyadh) Jan. 4, 1994.

38. Grace Halsell, *Prophesy and Politics* (Westport, CT: Laurence Hill, 1986); Dewey M. Beegle, *Prophesy and Prediction* (Ann Arbor, MI: Pryor Pettingill, 1978).

39. Fuad Sha'ban, *Islam and Arabs in Early American Thought* (Durham, NC: Acorn Press, 1991). Sha'ban explores the antecedents of contemporary millenarianism from the founding of Plymouth colony to Ulysses S. Grant.

40. William Tracy, "Mapping the Middle East in America", *Aramco World* Vol. 48, No. 6 November/December 1994 pp. 16-32.

41. See Georges C. Anawati, O.P., "An Assessment of the Christian-Islamic Dialogue", in Kail C. Ellis, ed., *The Vatican, Islam and the Middle East* (Syracuse, NY: Syracuse University Press, 1987). pp. 51-69 esp. pp. 53 ff. Other sources dealing with the broader problem of Vatican-Middle East politics and diplomacy are: George Emile Irani, *The Papacy and the Middle East: The Role of the Holy See in the Arab-Israeli Conflict*, 1962-1984 (Notre Dame, IN: University of Notre Dame Press, 1986). [Archbishop] Renato R. Martino, "The Holy See and the Middle East" *American-Arab Affairs* Summer 1989. No. 29 pp. 75-85.

42. His Holiness, John Paul II, *Crossing the Threshold of Hope* (New York: Alfred A. Knopf, 1994) pp. 91-143, esp. the chapter titled "Muhammad?", pp. 91-94.

43. *Ecclesiam Suam, Vatican II Encyclical Letter of Paul VI*, August 16. 1964. Text accessible in Claudia Carlen, ed., *The Papal Encyclicals* 1958-1981 (Raleigh, NC: McGrath Publishing Company, 1981.) pp. 135-160, esp. par. 107, p. 157.

44. *Lumen Gentium, Vatican II Encyclical Letter of Paul VI* 21 November 1964. Text accessible in Austin P. Flannery, ed., *Documents of Vatican II* (Grand Rapids, MI: William B. Eerdmans Publisher, 1975) pp. 350-423, esp. p. 367.

45. *Nostra Aetate, Vatican II Declaration* October 28, 1965. Text accessible in Flannery, ed., cited above in no. 44. pp. 739-740.

46. *Evangelii Nuntiandi, Vatican II Apostolic Exhortation of Paul VI* December 8, 1975. Text accessible in *The Teachings of Pope Paul VI - 1975* (Citta del Vaticano, Libreria Editrice Vaticana, 1975) pp. 506-566.

47. *Redemptoris Missio, Encyclical Letter of John Paul II,* December 7, 1990. Text accessible in William R. Burrows, ed., *Redemption and Dialogue* (Maryknoll, NY: Orbis Books, 1993) pp. 3-56.

48. *Evangelium Vitae, Encyclical Letter of John Paul II,* March 25, 1995. Text accessible in *Origins* (Catholic News Service) Vol. 24, No. 42, April 6, 1995 pp. 690-730.

49. See note 3 above.

50. See note 22 above.

51. As reported in James Zogby, "Countering the Campaign Against Islam in the U.S." *Arab News*, (Riyadh) July 12, 1993.

52. Robert H. Pelletreau, Jr.; Daniel Pipes; John L. Esposito; "Symposium: Resurgent Islam in the Middle East", *Middle East Policy*, Vol. III, No. 2, 1994, p. 3. See also Anthony Lake "Confronting Backlash States", *Foreign Affairs* Vol. 73, No. 2 March/April 1994, pp. 45-53, esp. p. 52, Charles W. Holmes, "U.S. Emphasizes It Isn't Anti-Islam", *Washington Times*, March 8, 1995.

53. William Pfaff, *The Wrath of Nations* (New York: Simon and Schuster, 1993) pp. 109-131, esp. 130-131; John Esposito, *Islamic Threat: Myth or Reality?* (London: Oxford University Press, 1932). For the Beedham article, see n. 22 above.

54. Dr. Abdul Qader Tash, "Islam in Britain", *Arab News* (Riyadh), July 10, 1994.

55. As quoted in *Arab News* (Riyadh), October 10, 1994.

56. See John Hicks and Paul Knitter, eds., *The Myth of Christian Uniqueness* (Maryknoll, NY: Orbis Books, 1988); Gavin D'Costa, ed., *Christian Uniqueness Reconsidered* (Maryknoll, NY: Orbis Books, 1990). See also Charles A. Kimball, *Striving Together: A Way Forward in Christian-Muslim Relations* (Maryknoll, NY: Orbis Books, 1990). These are examples of a more extensive literature.

57. *The New York Times*, January 29, 1991.

58. Spengler, cited above in n. 23. Vol II, p. 243. For general analysis of the tension between the concepts of the nation and Islamic doctrine, see James P. Piscatori, *Islam and the World of Nation-States* (Cambridge, England, Cambridge University Press, 1986).

59. Further description of these entities can be found in Ralph Braibanti, "Recovery of Islamic Identity in Global Perspective", Chapter 6 in Bruce Lawrence, ed., *The Rose and the Rock* (Durham, NC: Carolina Academic Press, 1979) pp. 159-165.

60. Peter Mansfield, *The New Arabians* (Chicago: Ferguson Publishing Company, 1981).

61. Two of the major books are John A. Sandwick, ed., *The Gulf Cooperation Council* (Boulder, CO: Westview Press, 1987); R.K. Ramazani and Joseph A. Kechichian, eds., *The Gulf Cooperation Council: Record and Analysis* (Charlottesville, VA: University of Virginia Press, 1988).

62. For an account of King Faisal's dedication to the Pan-Islamic cause see David E. Long, "King Faisal's World View", pp. 173-184; Abdullah M. Sindhi "King Faisal and Pan-Arabism", pp. 184-202; Ralph Braibanti, "Saudi-Arabia in the Context of Political Development Theory", pp. 35-58 -

all chapters in Willard A. Beling, ed., *King Faisal and the Modernization of Saudi Arabia* (London: Croom Helm, 1980). See also Ralph Braibanti, "Saudi Arabia: A Scholar's Perspective", *Al-Mubta'ath*, July 1989, pp. 82-89.

63. Harry F. Kern, "The Organization of the Islamic Conference", *American-Arab Affairs*, Spring 1987, No. 20, p. 104.

64. *Treaty Instituting the Maghreb Union*, 17 February 1989. Text accessible in *American-Arab Affairs* Winter 1989-90, No. 31, pp. 149-154.

65. *Agreement on the Establishment of the Arab Cooperation Council* February 16, 1989. Text accessible in *American-Arab Affairs* Spring 1989, No. 28, pp. 116-121.

66. This is explored further in Ralph Braibanti, "Introduction" in Kenneth E. Bauzon, *Liberalism and the Quest for Islamic Identity in the Philippines* (Durham, NC: Acorn Press, 1991) pp. xv-xx.

67. *Refugees*, (New York: The United Nations High Commission for Refugees, No. 4, 1994) p. 31.

68. See Zafar Ishaq Ansari, "Hijrah in the Islamic Tradition", in Ewan Anderson and Nancy Hatch Dupree, eds., *The Cultural Basis of Afghan Nationalism* (London: Pinter Publishers, 1990) pp. 3-20.

69. Said Azhar, "Afghan Refugees in Pakistan: A Pakistani View", in Anderson and Dupree, eds., cited above in n. 68 p. 109.

70. Garth N. Jones, "*Musjid* and *Istana*: Indonesia's Uneasy Calm in Its Developmentalist Age", *Journal of Third World Studies* Vol. 8, No. 2 Fall 1991, pp. 6-32.

71. Roy Mottahedeh, *The Mantle of the Prophet: Religion and Politics in Iran* (New York: Simon and Schuster, 1985) pp. 311-313.

72. Peter J. Chelkowski, "Ta'ziyeh: Indigenous Avant-Garde Theatre of Iran", p. 2 and Ehsan Yarshater "Ta'ziyeh and Pre-Islamic Mourning Rites in Iran", pp. 88-94 both in Peter J. Chelkowski, ed., *Ta'ziyeh: Ritual and Drama in Iran* (New York: New York University Press, 1979).

73. Richard V. Weekes, editor-in-chief, *Muslim Peoples: A World Ethnographic Survey* (Westport, CT: Greenwood Press, 1978).

74. For a survey of independence efforts see Robert Olson, "The Kurdish Question and Geopolitic and Geostrategic Changes in the Middle East After the Gulf War", *Journal of South Asian and Middle Eastern Studies*, Vol. XVII, No. 4, Summer 1994, pp. 44-67.

75. See comment and texts of treaties in Hafeez Malik, "Introduction to the Text of Twelve Agreements between Tatarstan and the Russian Federation", *Journal of South Asian and Middle Eastern Studies*, Vol. XVIII, No. 1, Fall 1994, pp. 61-94.

76. For discussion of alternative solutions see Iftikhar H. Malik, "Kashmir Dispute: A Stalemate or a Solution", *Journal of South Asian and Middle Eastern Studies*, Vol. XVI, No. 4 Summer 1993, pp. 55-72.

77. Charles Hamilton, *Hedaya or Guide: A Commentary on the Mussulman Laws* (Lahore: Premier Book House, 1957) Book XLII, p. 587

78. Further analysis can be found in Ralph Braibanti, "A Rational Context for Analysis of Arab Polities", *American Arab Affairs*, No. 21, Summer 1987, pp. 108-122.

79. Moncure Daniel Conway, *My Pilgrimage To The Wise Men of the East* (Boston: Houghton Mifflin, 1906) pp. 166, 249-250.

80. *First Things,* No. 28, February, 1993, p. 72.

81. Alija Ali Izetbegovic, *Islam Between East and West* (Indianapolis, IN: American Trust Publications, 1993) pp. xxxiii, 200. See also Mark Pinson, ed., *The Muslims of Bosnia-Herzegovina* (Cambridge, MA: Harvard University Press, 1994).

82. See a recent study, Mark R. Cohen, *Under Crescent and Cross: The Jews in the Middle Ages* (Princeton, NJ: Princeton University Press, 1994).

83. Judith Miller, "Faces of Fundamentalism", *Foreign Affairs* Vol. 73, No. 6, November/December 1994, pp. 123-144.

APPENDIX

ORGANIZATION OF THE ISLAMIC CONFERENCE
Established In 1969. Secretariat In Jeddah.
(As of 1995)

52 MEMBER STATES

Afghanistan	Indonesia	Palestine
Albania	Iran	Qatar
Algeria	Iraq	Saudi Arabia
Azerbaijan	Jordan	Senegal
Bahrain	Kuwait	Sierra Leone
Bangladesh	Kyrgyzstan	Somalia
Benin	Lebanon	Sudan
Brunei	Libya	Syria
Burkina Faso	Malaysia	Tajikistan
Cameroon	Maldives	Tunisia
Chad	Mali	Turkey
Comoros	Mauritania	Turkmenistan
Dijbouti	Morocco	Uganda
Egypt	Mozambique	United Arab
Gabon	Niger	Emirates
Gambia	Nigeria	Yemen
Guinea	Oman	Zanzibar
Guinea-Bissau	Pakistan	(Tanzania)

5 OBSERVER STATES

Bosnia & Herzegovina
Kazakstan
Moro Liberation Front

Turkish Muslim Community
of Cyprus
Uzbekistan

LEAGUE OF ARAB STATES
Established In 1945. Secretariat In Cairo.
(As of 1995)

22 MEMBER STATES

Algeria	Morocco
Bahrain	Oman
Comoros	Palestine
Djibouti	Qatar
Egypt*	Saudi Arabia*
Iraq*	Somalia
Jordan*	Sudan
Kuwait	Syria*
Lebanon*	Tunisia
Libya	United Arab Emirates
Mauritania	Yemen*

* Original founding states

AFTERWORD

Javeed Akhter, M.D.
Executive Director
International Strategy and Policy Institute

The International Strategy and Policy Institute (ISPI) was established in 1994 by a group of American Muslims in the Chicago area. Its objective is to promote correct understanding about Islam in the United States and to explain the moral and ethical positions of Islam. It seeks to bring those positions to bear on the formulation of public policy. The Institute is motivated by the belief that great nations like the United States should not just have interests but ideals. Islamic ideals promote justice and advocate a middle of the road approach and would be a positive influence on the United States and the world.

One of the means of achieving these ideals is the publication of position papers on selected topics of public policy in which Islamic solutions might play a constructive role. This essay by Professor Ralph Braibanti is the first of this series. A condensed version was delivered as a lecture at the Center for Middle Eastern Studies, University of Chicago, March 31, 1995. The essay is necessarily broad in scope as it seeks to establish the contextual framework for the subsequent papers. These will deal with the specific issues such as justice, environment, family values, personal health, spiritual life and relations between Islam and other religions particularly Judaism and Christianity. One basic objective of the Institute's efforts is to promote understanding and harmony among all the religious beliefs. Therefore the emphasis is on similarities of religious views and practices rather than on differences.

Muslims are approximately 27 percent of the world population, have a rich civilization and a distinctive perspective on life. They are a significant and growing minority in Europe and North America, yet they are not properly understood. Ignorance about Islam results in widespread stereotyping of Muslims frequently leading to racial and ethnic distortions. This first position paper is designed in part to stratify these misconceptions and offers methodologies for correcting them. Professor Braibanti's explanation of the origins of antagonism towards Islam and the distortions implicit in the term "fundamentalist" is a necessary first step in promoting an understanding of Islam in the West. Regrettably, distortions of Islam are not limited to popular culture but equally permeate scholarly literature as the work of Bernard Lewis and Samuel Huntington suggest. Even a cursory view of the Muslim world and Muslim history belies the notion that Muslims are violent extremists. From the Spanish Inquisition of 1492 to the current "ethnic cleansing" of Bosnian Muslims by Serbs, the massacres of Chechnya by the Russians, or the atrocities against Kashmiri Muslims by Indian security forces, Muslims have and continue to be victims rather than perpetrators of violence.

Knowledge of fundamental Islamic principles and moral values would clarify many misunderstandings. These moral values drive decisions that many Muslims make as individuals and are the ideals that guide policy in Muslim nations. These beliefs would be catalysts for equity and socio-economic justice and may stem moral decay in American society.

In an abbreviated form, these are the quintessentials of the Muslim belief system.

Muslims believe in one transcendental God, *Allah*. The belief in one God is called *Taw'hid*. The Arabic word Allah is grammatically unique as it has no derivatives. It is neither plural nor gender specific; thus it emphasizes that the one and only God is neither male nor female. God's omnipotence and omnipresence transcend space, time and gender.

While acknowledging the prophets of the old Testament and the prophethood but not the divinity of *Issa* (Jesus), Muslims believe that Muhammad, (peace be upon him - PBUH) was the final prophet of God. Muslims believe in the eternal message of their scripture, the Qur'an, and in the historical and theological relationship with other related scriptures especially the Old Testament and the Bible. The Qur'an was revealed to the Prophet Muhammad (PBUH) and remains the same today fourteen centuries later.

Muslims believe in individual responsibility and accountability. All humans start with a clean record and with the freedom and capacity to choose between right, *halal*, and wrong, *haram*. They are answerable for their own deeds without any intermediary between them and God. Through the Qur'an mankind is the recipient of divine wisdom and knowledge. Knowledge is glorified in Islam. The first word revealed to the Prophet was Read, *Iqra*. The acquiring, expanding and spreading of knowledge is considered a sacred duty.

Like many other faiths, Islam believes in devotion to one's parents, goodwill, kindness, forgiveness towards others and self restraint. However, the practice of self restraint is not to be stretched to the extent of practicing monastic life. It is recommended that individuals get married and that they participate fully in both the joys and tribulations of life on earth. The institution of marriage is at the core of family life of

Muslims. A Muslim marriage is a contract rather than a sacrament. Civility between spouses is mandated by the Qur'an and reinforced by the Prophet's own life. In case of marital discord arbitration and counseling is highly recommended. Divorce is permitted only as a last resort.

The same principles that govern private conduct between individuals also govern societies. The use of alcohol and drugs are forbidden as they are both personal addictions and are harmful to the society. Gambling enterprises including State lotteries are practically nonexistent.

Justice is another value that Islam emphasizes at the core of a healthy and peaceful society. Islam's messenger, Muhammad (PBUH), exhorted his followers to stop injustice actively or at the very least not to rationalize it. In extreme cases of injustice, Muslims believe in the right of self-defense. To struggle against an unjust cause or personal temptation is referred to as a *Jihad*. Jihad, unlike the Crusades, is not equivalent of Holy War. Jihad in the deepest sense is the eternal struggle in human life between good and evil forces.

Principles of justice and equality also govern gender and race relationships. Men and women are considered equal in the eyes of Allah. Religious responsibilities are largely the same for men and women; each must pray, fast, give alms and go on pilgrimage to Mecca. While men and women are seen as being equal, they are also seen as having distinct and complementary roles. Modesty of clothing and behavior is encouraged for both men and women. The intent is to create an environment in which the spiritual rather than the sensual qualities of men and women are given prominence. Over time, this idea has been corrupted by various cultural forces and has been made to appear as religious sanctions for discrimination against women. The concept of equality applies to all classes and races. A dramatic example of this is seen during the Muslim pilgrimage to Mecca called *Hajj* where all Muslims, rich and poor, black and white, wear the same clothing as a sign of universal brotherhood. This concept of racial equality is one of the most deeply rooted principles of Islam.

This egalitarianism and emphasis on human dignity carry on into the notion of self-respect and freedom from blasphemy and false accusations. In Muslim law the penalty for bringing a false accusation is as severe as the alleged crime. Human rights are an original Islamic concept. European crusaders learned principles of humane treatment of prisoners of war from their contact with Islamic jurisprudence.

Muslim jurisprudence is based on rights and principles called the *Shar'ia*. Individuals have a right to life, dignity, family, knowledge, property and freedom from coercion in matters of religion. Crimes are regarded as violations of divine law not human law. Islamic punishments (*Hudud*) have received much criticism in the West for being harsh. These punishments are effective because they are tempered by a rigid judicial process and by compassion, forgiveness and general God-consciousness in the society. Even in the case of the death penalty for murder, relatives of the victim are encouraged to forgive and accept fair restitution. Islam believes strongly in the sanctity of human life and does not allow for its destruction including suicide and most cases of abortion.

In Muslim law the right to own property and generate wealth is tempered by an acute sense of fair dealing, equitable distribution of wealth and socioeconomic justice. One of the major tenets of Islam is *Zakat*, a compulsory sharing of wealth with needy members of the society. A productive economy free of exploitation is required and encouraged.

Concerning public polity Islam stipulates only the guiding principles of "government by the righteous" and "governance by consultation." No specific governmental structure is recommended. The result is a wide spectrum of political systems. As Islam is a holistic belief system there is no separation between church and state.

The prevailing perceptions of Islam in the West are so unfair and divorced from reality that Muslims understandably feel frustrated. The result is cynicism, anger, and a tendency for Muslims to isolate themselves. If the media gave more attention to educating themselves and the public about the fundamentals of Islam through presentations like Dr. Braibanti's paper rather than chasing such phantoms as "fundamentalism," "green menace" and "Muslim rage," we could begin to reverse some of these erroneous perceptions. Many western paradigms do not apply to Muslim societies. "Fundamentalism" and "holy war" are both western paradigms with no equivalence in Islam. Extremism in many Muslim countries should be understood for what it is, namely a reaction to repressive dictatorial regimes. An unbiased and balanced study of Muslims would be the morally correct and intellectually honest stance that would further bond Muslims and the countries that they have chosen to live in. Thus, the richness and rectitude of the Muslim value system would contribute positively to the maintenance of a just and harmonious social order. As Dr. Braibanti points out, ". . . at this moment in history the dynamics and clearly defined values of Islam have the potential for resuscitating the western world's decline to morbidity."

ABOUT THE AUTHOR

The Institute is fortunate to have its first position paper written by so distinguished a scholar as Dr. Ralph Braibanti, James B. Duke Professor of Political Science Emeritus at Duke University. Before joining the Duke faculty in 1953, Professor Braibanti taught at Kenyon College and served as assistant director of the American Political Science Association in Washington, D.C. During World War II he was a military government officer in the occupation of Japan.

From 1960 to 1962 he was advisor to the Civil Service Academy of Pakistan. His studies of the judicial and administrative systems of Pakistan have been widely acclaimed. The government of Pakistan in 1987 published a collection of his writings under the title *Evolution of Pakistan's Administrative System The Collected Papers of Ralph Braibanti.* He is the author of more than a hundred major scholarly articles and several books including *Research on the Bureaucracy of Pakistan;* and is editor and co-author of *Administration and Economic Development in India; Asian Bureaucratic Systems Emergent from the British Imperial Tradition; Pakistan: the Long View; Tradition, Values and Socio-Economic Development,* and *Political and Administrative Development.* Subsequently he served as Ford Foundation consultant in Lebanon and Saudi Arabia, U.N. consultant in Malaysia, UNESCO consultant in Morocco, World Bank consultant on Bangladesh and visiting professor at the University of Kuwait.

In 1989 he was appointed King Faisal Distinguished International Lecturer in Islamic Affairs by the Arab-American Affairs Council (now the Middle East Policy Council).

At Duke University he established the program in Islamic and Arabian Development Studies and was its director until his retirement in 1990. He was awarded the Alumni Distinguishing Teaching Award and the Student Body's Designation as Distinguished Teacher. He received the Ph.D. degree from Syracuse University, and holds the honorary degree of Doctor of Humane Letters from Western Connecticut State University where he was an undergraduate.

J.A.